Mirrors of War

Mirrors of War

Literature and Revolution in El Salvador

Edited by
Gabriela Yanes,
Manuel Sorto,
Horacio Castellanos Moya,
Lyn Sorto

Translated by Keith Ellis

MONTHLY REVIEW PRESS
NEW YORK

Library of Congress Cataloging in Publication Data

Fragmentos de la actual literatura Salvadoreña. English.
   Mirrors of War.
   Translation of: Fragmentos de la actual literatura
   Salvadoreña.
   1. Salvadoran literature — 20th century.   2. Revolutionary
   literature, Salvadoran.   I. Yanes, Gabriela.   II. Title.
   PQ7535.F7313   1985   860   85-13890
   ISBN 0-85345-687-9 (pbk.)

Monthly Review Press
155 West 23rd Street, New York, N.Y. 10011

Printed in Canada

10 9 8 7 6 5 4 3 2 1

Contents

INTRODUCTION
by Keith Ellis

For more than a decade the small Central American country of El Salvador has been in a state of war. At the core of the conflict the ruling oligarchy and military are ranged against a coalition of forces struggling for the rights and good of the people in general. The war, with deep roots in Salvadorean history, has taken a toll of more than 50,000 lives in the first half of the 1980s alone.

During the 1970s, when opposition movements had mounted a growing challenge in the form of clandestine activities, the military dictatorship responded with terror. The traditional armed forces were supplemented by death-squads and paramilitary gangs adept at perpetrating disappearances, torture, and killings, all calculated to elicit compliance from the civilian population. By the end of the decade Salvadoreans faced several alternatives: to acquiesce in the brutality, to go on living in helpless fear, to seek refuge in remote parts of the country or in other countries, or to join in a guerrilla war of liberation.

Salvadorean writers are overwhelmingly among the resisters. Like others in opposition, writers who oppose the regime have been exiled either to underground activity or to other countries. They find themselves committed to a war aimed at establishing popular democracy, to superseding unrepresentative elections based on threats and fear. They are committed to the participation of all the country's people in the national life, to putting an end to terror and carnage.

In many parts of the world the war has been distorted, seen through the warped lenses of political leaders, media, and other advocates of the status quo: spokespeople who convey the impression that "fair elections" are possible in a military-run country living through a constant state of war, where the real opposition is not only denied access to the electoral system but also to any open communication with the public.

The Carter and Reagan administrations have taken an intense national struggle for justice and put it on the international stage through increasing U.S. involvement. (In late 1984 El Salvador's President José Napoléon Duarte said the United States government was spending $1 million a day on the war.) Ronald Reagan insistently waves the flag of anti-communism before his fellow Americans, and, as in the cases of Grenada and Nicaragua, the intellects and consciences of large numbers of them go to sleep. The legitimate claims of the opposition are distorted into an East-West issue, a Soviet-Cuban plot. A twisted view of U.S. national interest becomes the entire cruel focus; and the history of the Salvadorean people is thus swept aside.

This dominant — and dismaying — image of the Salvadorean war is contested by the writing in *Mirrors of War*, which was compiled in its original Spanish in the early 1980s. The poetry, prose, and testimony here are a form of direct and creative response to the Salvadorean dilemma, to the ongoing bitter conflict. The work recasts the distortions, presenting a rectifying view of an embattled society from the other side of the front-line. This radically different picture of the society from the pens of its writers and poets mirrors the lives of the people in their everyday conflicts: their voices, fears, hopes, sorrows, and determination to understand and fight against an unjust system.

The compilers of this collection, four Salvadoreans living in exile, speak of it as a "cinematographic edition" rather than a chronological or genre-based selection.[1] I take this to mean that the pieces, if read in succession, capture the unfolding images of the war: its historical roots, its physical and psychological effects on the people, the conditions the guerrillas seek to change, the U.S. presence, torture and death-squad activity, guerrilla action. The pieces look at the consequences of the war for literature, for the church, for the peasants who make up the regime's Special Forces, for friendships, and for the class structure. Read sensitively, the collection may be seen as a revolutionary presentation of a powerful new body of literature that mirrors the Salvadorean peoples' quest for change.

The literature and the conflict that inspires it are the culmination of a history that goes back to the meeting on unequal terms of conquered and conqueror, of the indigenous and Spanish peoples. The term "conquest" is applicable to the whole colonial project, including, in its violent connotation, the acts involved in spawning a new mestizo, or mixed, population. The country's independence, declared in 1821, was followed by a dramatic revolt in 1833 of both Indian and mestizo peasants, who seized the alcaldía and overthrew their creole landlords. The peasant army won a number of victories before the republican authorities were able to overcome it in "a bloody repressive campaign."[2] The Indian leader Anastasio Aquino, in effect El Salvador's first rebel hero, was captured and executed.

The oligarchical control of a basic asset, land, was tightened in the post-Independence period. The Land Laws of 1881-82 did away with what remained of the communal lands that the Indians had been allowed to keep in colonial times. This chronic and worsening deprivation prompted more peasant rebellions in the late nineteenth and early twentieth centuries, leading finally to the uprising of Indians and mestizos led by Farabundo Martí in 1932. The result was the slaughter of 30,000 peasants by the army and a new martyrdom, that of Farabundo Martí.

Since that time the oligarchy has been ruthless in its tenacity. Some two per cent of the population holds sixty per cent of the arable lands, with the consequent widespread social ills: an illiteracy rate of more than forty per cent, an infant mortality rate of sixty-three for every thousand live births, malnutrition affecting more than seventy per cent of children under five years old, and widespread absence of medical care. The intervention of reformers, certain sectors of the Catholic church prominent among them, was met with unyielding repression and violence, directed for the most part against the civilian population. As a result, most Salvadoreans desiring change have, however uneasily, decided to undertake revolutionary armed struggle.

One of the most notable victims of the war was the Archbishop of San Salvador, Oscar Arnulfo Romero. Observing the brutal treatment suffered by the peasants and the poor of the cities, Romero decided that it was impossible to serve God without defending those people. Calling himself "the voice of the voiceless," he stated that "Christian faith requires that we submerge ourselves in the world." He went on to dedicate himself to the practice of what is called liberation theology; and for this he was murdered as he said mass on the evening of March 24, 1980.

In August 1984 Romero's successor, the Archbishop Arturo Rivera y Damas, condemned the escalating supply of arms to the government by foreign powers, and the bombings of civilians who had fled to remote areas of the country. He asked instead that these powers help to relieve the suffering of the Salvadorean people. Priests and poets, guerrilla and revolutionary political leaders (most of them members of groupings that have united to form the FMLN — the Farabundo Martí National Liberation Front — and the FDR — the Democratic Revolutionary Front) have called for talks to end the warfare on terms that will protect and further the interests of the people at large.

Literature is crucially involved in this movement for political change. In this respect what is happening in El Salvador reflects the historical relationship between literature and society in other parts of Spanish America. During the colonial period, Spanish American literature represented, sometimes by force of law, the interests of the colonizers. If the writers in the decades following the independence movement of the early nineteenth century came from the privileged class, as cultural guardians of the new republics they concerned themselves in a general way with the well-being of Spanish America. Yet late in the century the astute observer José Martí noted that the spirit of the colonies had continued in the republics and that as a step forward common cause should be made with the most exploited sectors of the population.

This common cause has been joined more and more in our century, particularly in Central America and the Caribbean, and with profound revolutionary ramifications. The great work of Cuba's Nicolás Guillén is a special example of this; and the lead of Nicaragua's Ernesto Cardenal in writing on behalf of the oppressed has been followed by many in Central America. With the impetus towards political change has come a steady tide of literature, produced by people who unreservedly dedicate their talents to the revolutionary struggle and want their poems, novels, short stories, and testimonies to serve as tools in the building of a radically different society.[3]

This dedication hardly seems to come out of a self-conscious decision to write socially committed literature. It reflects, rather, the absorbing, preoccupying, inescapable impact of a brutal, oligarchical repression clashing with a people's aspiration to social, economic, and political justice.

The adjective "rebel" applies to the literature produced in such circumstances, in the sense that there is the rejection of a ruling governmental system. The adjective "guerrilla" may also be applied in the sense that the writings often deal with the actual war against the system and the writers may be active participants in combat, in the tradition of Ernesto Che Guevara, Peru's Javier Heraud, or Guatemala's Otto René Castillo. Or the adjective "revolutionary" may be appropriate in the sense that the literature conveys a firm will to implement a vision of a new society. It may actually be produced from liberated areas which, while not altogether secure, are prototypes for the generally sought aims.[4]

There is more and more evidence in Central America and the Caribbean of the convergence of all three adjectives, along with others such as "militant" and "subversive," to describe a new stage of socially committed literature. All of these words might well be subsumed under the word "revolutionary."

The revolutionary writers who address themselves to the pressing and relievable burdens of their compatriots are inclined to employ expressive forms notable for their simplicity. They capture the rhythms and diction of popular speech, and their imagery is rooted in the experiences and way of life of the people. They make it clear that the combination of social concern and respectful appreciation of the artistic possibilities of the expressive modes of the people can achieve the dignity and majesty of poetry.

Another important factor in the creation of simple authenticity is the prominence of the first-person narrator. This device not only connects the reader to a certain existing consciousness but also gives a documentary character to the writings, whether they be lyric poems, short stories, novels, or literally, testimonies. And since a society in a state of upheaval produces many voluble witnesses, there is an explosion of creative talent despite the difficult obstacles to publication imposed by hostile regimes. In Nicaragua, for example, the struggle against the Somoza dictatorship spawned a host of new writers and some new publications.[5] Ernesto Cardenal figured importantly in the roles of producer, guide, and encourager, establishing thereby the credentials for his present position as Minister of Culture in the Sandinista government.

The characteristics of revolutionary literature are well illustrated by the work of Salvadorean writers. When José Roberto Cea published his *General Anthology of Poetry in El Salvador* inside the country in 1971, he included twenty-two poets beginning with Francisco Gavidia (1863-1955), a contemporary and friend of the great Nicaraguan poet, Rubén Darío. The anthology thus shows the eclecticism and formal concerns that characterized Salvadorean poetry during Gavidia's lifetime. Cea wrote of a "poetry of underdevelopment, of people dependent on the cultural expression of other countries. The poetry written in our country followed standards experienced elsewhere, in France and Spain, particularly."[6]

Nevertheless, some of the poets included in Cea's anthology (eight of those poets contribute to *Mirrors of War*) were already revealing the will to intensify the relationship between literature and society. The University of El Salvador Literary Circle was founded in 1956 by the Salvadoreans Roque Dalton, Manlio Argueta, and Roberto Armijo, and the Guatemalan Otto René Castillo. Since, as Dalton put it, poetry is written with more than words, the Circle decided to confront comprehensively the tradition of dictatorship and repression in Central America, using literature as one of their weapons. The relatively peaceful period of the late 1960s to the early 1970s permitted the publication within El Salvador of many of the works of writers who came to reflect the view of the Circle.

But 1972 ended all hope of peaceful change. That year a hard-fought election resulted in victory for a coalition led by José Napoleón Duarte and Guillermo Ungo. The new government lasted only half a day, before the army handed power over to one of its own, Colonel Molina. Thereafter, as military and paramilitary forces took open control of the administration and repression became more wanton, writers were obliged to publish their works outside of the country. Not only did the authors have their views of the world and of poetry intensified by developments in El Salvador, but the number of literary producers also grew, with several new collections appearing in a variety of formats.

Some of these collections include *Homage to El Salvador*, published in Madrid in 1981, with an introduction by Claribel Alegría and a prologue by Julio Cortázar.[7] It contains poems by both Salvadoreans (most of them represented in *Mirrors*) and non-Salvadoreans such as the veteran Spanish poets Rafael Alberti and José Bergamín. Another collection is *El Salvador: People's Poetry Eighty-Two*, published in London (no publication date), with mostly anonymous poems giving the effect of representative voices arising from a collective struggle. Similar to this last book is *El Salvador: Poems of Rebellion* (undated), with a prologue by Julio Cortázar, published by Blackrose Press, London. The same publishers have focused on selections from the work of Roque Dalton in the collection *El Salvador: Militant Poetry* (undated).[8]

The anthology *Contemporary Central American Poetry*, published in Spain in 1983 and edited by Roberto Armijo and Rigoberto Paredes, presents work by forty-one poets (born between 1900 and 1950) from El Salvador, Guatemala, Honduras, Nicaragua, and Costa Rica.[9] By so doing it illustrates the different political stages reached by the various interrelated countries. In his introductory essay Armijo contrasts the secure and officially encouraged flourishing of the Nicaraguan literary scene with the precarious and heroic existence of writers from El Salvador and Guatemala. In this regard Armijo, a Salvadorean (Paredes is from Honduras), writes:

> *The regimes that rule our countries at present are removing all opportunities from Central American writers and poets. Fascism in El Salva-*

> *dor and Guatemala has put an end to some beau-*
> *tiful cultural experiences. In both countries many*
> *poets have been murdered or have fallen in com-*
> *bat against successive military regimes.*[10]

The Salvadorean poets included in the Armijo-Paredes collection are well represented in *Mirrors of War.*

Finally, there is Manlio Argueta's useful anthology, *Poetry of El Salvador* (published in Costa Rica in 1983.)[11] Like Cea's it begins with the nineteenth-century founders and continues with chronological representation through the first half of the twentieth century. But, reflecting the volume and quality of his national poetry, more than half of the works included were written after 1960. Chronology in this case demonstrates the increasing depth of maturity with which Salvadorean poets explore social questions, and here again there is an evident, and growing, tendency for Salvadorean poets to identify themselves with the cause of the oppressed majority of their fellow citizens. There are twenty of Argueta's poets — mainly the younger ones — among the forty writers in *Mirrors of War.*

Unlike the previous collections, selections from novels and prose testimonies play an important role in this book. But the principal difference here is the intense focus provided by the Salvadorean war; hence the title *Mirrors of War: Literature and Revolution in El Salvador.* The compilers have disclaimed any intention of preparing a general anthology of Salvadorean literature conveying a variety of high points of contemporary Salvadorean literature. Instead, the revolutionary struggle for a popular democracy in El Salvador serves as the nexus of the selections, as the factor that engages the sensibility of the writers.

When the compilers, in explaining the absence from these pages of writers who might be considered to be representative of Salvadorean literature, describe the collection modestly as "a partial, limited, and somewhat makeshift sample of Salvadorean writing in recent years," they are recognizing the special place of the war and its disruption, which precludes any hope of completeness. Secondly, the focus on the war brings with it a certain selectivity, especially so in the images of horror and hope, desperation and resolve.

As a result of this focus, there are certain omissions. A prominent poet like Oswaldo Escobar Velada (1919-61) is not represented even though his poetry denouncing social injustice has had a great impact on the work of several poets included here. At the same time, other renowned writers are represented only by compositions that reflect the new militancy. For this reason some of the most anthologized poems of Claudia Lars and Roque Dalton will not be found here. Rather, they are both represented by compositions written in the 1970s (*Poesía última 1970-1973* and *Poemas clandestinos*, respectively) in which the war has the clearest presence. Moreover, Dalton's well-known poem "Para un mejor amor" ("Everybody agrees that sex") appears here with the omission of the stanza that deals with sex in the context of "conventional" family life, a style of life not so common in the state of war. And whereas in the 1970s Dalton wrote a poem, "La guerra de guerrillas en El Salvador" ("Guerrilla warfare in El Salvador"), the poem "Acaxual" by the younger poet Roberto Quesada represents that topic here. This is perhaps because, other factors being equal, Quesada's poem refers instructively to the tactics of guerrilla warfare.

The intimacy with the war natural to the younger poets accounts for the fact that more than half of the writers who make up this collection were born after 1945. Some of these have been killed or have disappeared. The rest, like their surviving elders, are either living in exile (for the most part in Mexico, Nicaragua, or Costa Rica) or fighting as guerrillas in El Salvador. The poet Eduardo Sancho Castañeda appeared on television in many countries in late 1984 when as Comandante Fermán Cienfuegos he served as a spokesperson for the FMLN in the first of a series of talks with the Duarte regime.

There is an element of historical chronology in the presentation of the scenes in this book as they unfold before the reader. Thus, after the initial poem in which Claribel Alegría provides, not without humour, a sketch of the historical and social constituents of El Salvador, the scene shifts to a view, informed by present-day guerrilla consciousness, of the sixteenth-century Spanish conquest of the indigenous and ingenuous Salvadorean people. The early selections also reveal an attachment to the Indian population (indicative of the current search for the popular foundations of Salvadorean culture) culminating in depictions of Anastasio Aquino, the nineteenth-century Indian martyr, and the Indian uprisings of 1833. The writers convey this attachment through the use of authentic Salvadorean speech, including colloquialisms and words from the Nahual Indian language.

Claribel Alegría's narrative brings us to 1932, the modern era of massacre by machine-gun, while Claudia Lars provides a brief portrait of a slaughtered but productive Indian peasant and Mercedes Durand gives the antithetical picture of the organizer of the repressive system, who is again seen from a similar perspective in Alfonso Hernández's poem.

José María Cuéllar's poem examines the question of ancestry, with a powerful sentiment that denounces the original sexual violence against Indian women and the continuing social violence. The picture of social chaos, presented through the multiple roles of the collective woman, and conveyed by the frantic prose rhythm of Manlio Argueta's first piece in the collection, brings us to the El Salvador of the 1970s and 1980s. And Argueta's second piece, the first of two selections from his renowned novel *Un día en la vida* (*One Day of Life*, 1983) reveals one of the central horrors of these times: the Salvadorean trained to despise and terrorize his own people.[12] Argueta, superbly handling the technique of first-person dramatic monologue in both pieces, reveals the bizarre consciousness of an estranged, revved-up, and menacing representative of the regime's Special Forces. The following poems offer scenes of terror, absurdity, and desperate armed reaction.

Another distinctive feature of this collection is the remarkable number of poems dealing with poetry itself. Several poems are devoted to the idea of the role of the writer in a brutal society. Claudia Lars (1899-1974), for instance, ranks with the finest of poets in Spanish America, admired for her dedication to art and to poets notwithstanding her comfortable economic situation. Her poetry in her last years came to reflect the horror and grief of her surroundings. Thus the poem:

> *Wounded by machine-guns*
> *the innocent one lay forgetting his fright*
> *in his modest coffin.*
> *Contemplating him I lost forever*
> *my seventy-year-old infancy.*

Róger Lindo's poem, following this one, is a subtle and metaphorically rich exploration of the growth from introspection to social commitment; and immediately thereafter different poems and prose narratives offer indications of the precariousness of survival and instances of the terror that compel social awareness in the writer. The most notorious case is the murder of Archbishop Romero, represented here in a poem by Alfonso Quijada Urías. Roque Dalton probes the relationship between war and creativity, addresses the new political consciousness of women, and traces the development of the war itself in three poems, while Manuel Sorto illustrates the pragmatic role of metaphor in circumstances of war. In the rest of the book the writers are in a state of heightened eloquence in poems and prose pieces that deal with the war. Elements from the surrealistic to the folkloric, from the repulsive to the tender, function with absorbing effect.

The scenes in this book, thrown up from the struggles of the Salvadorean people, are a measure of the deep involvement of literature in the attempt to rectify the national life. The writers have made common cause with both the victims of oppression and those fighting for the country's freedom. They have immersed themselves in the popular values of their country, bringing a new understanding of the historical roots of the present suffering. The focus on the war itself facilitates coherence and provides a wide range of experiences. The work of this large and growing number of writers, in its cumulative effect, conveys a reality that is so painful a part of contemporary human experience that in the name of humanity it must be ended soon, with justice served.

FOREWORD TO THE SPANISH EDITION

We began this collection with only a general idea in mind: to publish a book that would in some way display the literature produced in El Salvador in the most recent years; a literature that springs from a social process that continues in the revolutionary war. At first we had no clear conception of the form we would give to this book; we did not even know whether the collected materials would be adequate (with regard to both quality and quantity) to make up a book.

We began trying to gather the largest possible number of works by Salvadorean writers. This was not an easy task, because the majority of young authors had no access to the sparse publication media and, besides, we were living in Mexico. The only alternative was to rely on friends, on comrades, to provide us with material they had managed to salvage from the turbulence of a country in a state of war, with those writings achieved literally in "the repose of the warrior."

This book would not have been possible without the collaboration of several comrades (we are especially grateful for the efforts of Oscar Soles and Romeo Galdámez) who searched for poems, short stories, song lyrics, and so on. Thus the collective work began. But at the same time one of the limitations of the book became obvious, or rather, came to be defined: the book is not a general anthology of Salvadorean literature or even a general anthology of revolutionary literature in El Salvador. We would perhaps call this book "a partial, limited, and somewhat makeshift sample of Salvadorean writing in recent years." It should not be surprising, then, that some of the writers who might be considered to be representative of our literature are not included in these pages.

The structure of the book could not therefore be submitted to the traditional canons of literary anthologies.

The idea then came to us to organize the material more as a "cinematographic edition" than as a chronological classification or by genres. There was, of course, a large area of subjectivity, of search. Given the nature of the task, this approach seemed to us to be the most appropriate.

We insisted that the literary quality of the materials should correspond with our criteria; taking into account, of course, the fact that we are — to a large degree — young writers, coming out of a society engulfed in war and therefore susceptible to pamphlets and their substitutes. On the other hand we were not inhibited by literary prejudices from having recourse to testimonies or newspaper articles.

With this book we hope to contribute new elements for a greater understanding of the Salvadorean people through our present literature, which like all aspects of our national life is deeply caught up in the whole process of the war.

Gabriela Yanes
Manuel Sorto
Horacio Castellanos Moya
Lyn Sorto

Mexico, 1982

Tamales from Cambray
Claribel Alegría

To Eduardo and Helena
who asked me for a
Salvadorean recipe

Two pounds of mestizo dough
half a pound of Gachupin loin
cooked and finely ground
a little box of Sister of Charity raisins
two spoonfuls of Malinche milk
one cup of seething water
lightly fried conquistador helmets
three Jesuit onions
a purse of multinational gold
two dragon's teeth
a big presidential carrot
two spoonfuls of informers
Panchimalco Indian lard
two ministerial tomatoes
half a cup of television sugar
two drops of volcano lava
seven pito leaves
(don't be evil-minded it is sleep-inducing)
put it all to simmer
on a low heat
for five hundred years
and you'll see what a flavour!

The Battle of Acaxual
Roberto Quesada

ACAXUAL
City washed by waves,
8 JUNE
1524
(well into the sixteenth century).

Pedro de Alvarado
(alias
Tonatiuh)
almost lost his breeches
when he saw he had only
a hundred cavalrymen
and a hundred and two horses,
a hundred and fifty white infantry men
and more or less
six thousand Indian auxiliaries.

Against a plain
teeming with natives,
thousands
with slingshots and clumps of earth in their hands,

ALSO SPEARS

And you, what did you say?
that with clumps of earth in our hands
they were going to seize us?

        Tonatiuh
        studied the situation
        and ordered his men
        to withdraw quietly and slowly.

The Acaxualian comrades
lacking military training
in their schools
trailed stupidly behind them
waiting for the enemy to stop.
But the man in command (Tonatiuh)
didn't raise his hand to signal "STOP,"
then the whole flock of Acaxualians
said to themselves that Tonatiuh
was a sissy.

        Tonatiuh got angry
        and told his men
        "about turn"
        or
        to turn around
        and fight.

For he knew that the Indians
(big-nosed and cross-eyed)
were already far from the mountain
close by Acaxual.

And they turned around!
the bastards
began to strike out in all directions with
spear thrusts,
stones,
kicks,
bites,
insults,
etc.,
etc.

IT WAS ONE BIG MESS.

The Indians also
made a mess...
the brawl was such
that when it ended
not a single Acaxualian
was left alive...

But they clobbered
quite a few on the other side,
there were many
maimed and broken,
and among the multitude with arrow wounds
was Tonatiuh.

How gallant, how gallant!
the dying were saying:
die,
die,
virgin of the cave.

People say
that the comrade who cured Tonatiuh
was a very good person
because she did no end of things to him
so he would limp for the rest of his life.

And that is how it was,
his left foot
(the one for scoring goals)
became quite lame,
on the lucky limb
he had to use
a sole ten layers thick.

But up until around February
of the following year,
Tonatiuh was
almost pushing up rubber trees,
confined to his sleeping mat,
between his bed and the grave.

I CONGRATULATE
ATONAL (R.I.P.)
(Alias
WATER SUN)
PERSONALLY
AND
MOST PARTICULARLY
for his hot blood,
but I advise him
next time,
TO AIM FOR THE MIDDLE OF THE CHEST.

(Song) from A Play Without a Name
Dimas Castellón-Mariano Espinoza

They brought their god
and with the cross
and with the cross
they cut off heads

They destroyed
our cities
and seized
the gold and jade

Where is the song
Where is the jade
Where is the land
and the happiness

I no longer work singing
a tithe for the church
and a fifth for the king
a tithe for the church
and a fifth for the king.

To them belong the fruits
and to us only hunger

FIRST PARCEL
José Roberto Cea

The few people who talk about my country
confuse it with a province of Brazil
or with the first land where Columbus set foot
when he discovered the New World.

from EREGUAYQUIN
Roberto Torres

There was once a city here
with its four cardinal points
that joyfully welcomed each May
and offered its finest grain to the god of corn
and pottery flourished with jugs for drinking chocolate
and pitchers held the vital water.

from CONCERNING ANASTASIO MARTYR AND HIS MOST CONFUSED HISTORY
Manuel Sorto

...and I started to remember how I came to know Martyr Anastasio Aquino and what I knew about him, and I went back to my village, to my education in public school, in college, in the institute, in the history they taught me, in which the indigenous people seemed like a bunch of ignoramuses, with murderous instincts and absurd or aberrant superstitions, who only thanks to the Spaniards who made them civilized and to the holymothercatholic-apostolicandromanchurch that had endowed them with a soul, today we know something about reading and writing. (Of course I heard my father say several times that "we come from pure Spanish stock, so watch it".) The heroes were the rascal Alvarado and the Corteses and the Pizarros and their mob of mystifiers who brought little mirrors and an enormous iron cross they used to split open coconuts and skulls, and as if that were not enough, they brought an unquenchable thirst for gold, which was comparable only to their equally unquenchable sexual appetite; heroes of death, rape, and looting. More than any national author, history painted them with halos of saints about their very narrow heads. What history!

And they told me that the Indians here had become extinct, with the exception of a small band that still survived over near Izalco; that there are still some in Mexico, Peru, or in Guatemala and so on and so forth. That history never said anything about the Nonualco people and Anastasio Aquino and their rebellion which took place hardly ten years after the declaration of the so much talked-of and distorted Central American independence. That history never said anything about the Izalcos and Feliciano Ama and how they came very close to being exterminated in 1932. Nor was it explained that the peasants who on Thursdays and on weekends filled the square, the market, and the arcades of the town and who brought the rope they made from agave fibre and made the pots in which the beans that fed us were cooked and which were the remains of a genetic creative ability that had its roots in one of the most complete and impressive cultures to have populated the planet: they did not explain, I repeat, they have never explained that those peasants were descendants of those Indians.

I never saw or heard in that history of the Indian any reference to art, or science, or much less to Anastasio Aquino or anything of the sort. And I was already graduating and on the way, it might be supposed, to becoming an honourable and know-it-all professional who would bolster the vital forces of the country. No, there was no Anastasio Aquino, only at the entrance to the capital, the statue of a faded Atlacatl which, symbolically, was erected on the street that is most notorious for public prostitution, and which besides is called Independence Avenue (I later learned that Atlacatl was nothing more than another invention). Yes, the history they educated me with was bogus, slanted, and corrupted. It all amounted to a farce, that left nothing but a profound cramp in my brain, my stomach, and my soul. It was emptiness, confusion... but also transition.

Today HISTORY is being built. We know that the Indian is alive and prepared; that he couldn't be annihilated in 1833 with Anastasio Aquino, nor a hundred years later. Anastasio rises constantly from ashes that are never extinguished, ready to recover his land and his dignity; ready to reconstruct his culture and his people.

from Rebel Song for Anastasio Martyr
with a Background of Whistles and Drums
Jaime Suárez Quemain

When the history of this country comes to be written,
        the true history,
the one that started with you, Martyr Anastasio,
        Commander General
of the Liberating Army of Santiago Nonualco,
when the time comes for knocking down statues,
for the putting an end to all the mythology
that little by little they engraved on our faces,
then Anastasio, Commander,
your name will be spoken...

from *ORGANIZED POETRY*
Róger Lindo

A breaker tonight
and fragments wash ashore from a strange village
inhabited by men who are all travellers
free because of love
toward an ancient
united
heroic
people

(Song) from A Play Without a Name
Dimas Castellón-Mariano Espinoza

Over there in the hills
ten thousand and more
white sombreros
are coming down

Coarse cotton trousers
and sharpened machetes

The peasants
evicted
evicting
are coming now

Over there in the hills
ten thousand and more
white sombreros
are coming down

from *IZALCO ASHES*
Claribel Alegría

Enveloped in an eerie calm, I continued walking toward
Izalco. Nothing moved along the highway; there were no
peasants working in the coffee fields; the huts I passed
were shut up, with no children playing outside or women
grinding coffee. Nevertheless, I felt that I was being observed, that I was being spied on from among the dried
brushwood.

There were soldiers on guard at each street corner of
the town and a reserve squad in the central square. Bullets had slashed yellow wounds into the white walls of
the houses. On the streets there were dark blotches
formed, it seemed, by dried blood. Except for the presence of the soldiers, I sensed the same silence, the same
suspension of daily activities that I had felt along the road.

The headquarters were in the mayor's office, opposite
the entrance to the church with its single whitewashed
tower. I handed my passport to one of the guards. After
a few minutes he showed me into the office, where the
captain was seated at his desk.

I repeated my story, once more omitting the details of
my escape. The captain listened without comment, nod-
ding his assent as I spoke.

"I must go immediately to Santa Ana," I told him. "How
can I manage that?"

He shrugged.

"All the buses and trucks have been requisitioned by the army," he informed me. "The public transportation network has still not yet been re-established. I'm very sorry I can't help you."

I asked him if I could go to Santa Ana in one of his vehicles. He refused flatly.

"I'm very sorry," he told me, "but only the army and the civil guard can use them."

"Isn't it possible to rent a private car, a horse, anything?" I insisted.

He became impatient.

"Everything has been requisitioned by the army," he repeated. "I can't go against orders. This is a military zone, mister, and until calm is restored it would be very dangerous for you to attempt to leave town."

He gave me back the passport and the interview ended.

I went out into the street to walk around in the hope of finding some way of getting to Santa Ana. With the exception of the soldiers there was not a soul in the streets. The people of Izalco were shut up in their houses, behind closed doors and windows, waiting.

It was six o'clock when I went to the tavern. There were a few soldiers standing in front of the bar chatting. Others, seated at a table, were taciturn, infected by the silence of Izalco. They looked fixedly at their glasses and only at long intervals would they softly say something. When I entered they looked at me curiously, but they paid no further attention to me nor I to them.

I headed for a corner where there was a single small table, and asked the old lady to bring me a bottle of beer.

The square of Izalco, almost deserted the previous day, was teeming with people. I noticed that various groups of soldiers were guarding the intersections; I felt apprehensive on seeing so many Indians with their straw hats and wide cotton trousers, leaning against walls, or squatting on the pavement stones. They were all without their machetes. The soldiers seemed not to be paying them any attention.

I headed for the outskirts of town, making my way through a wave of white shirts that now covered the road along which I had come yesterday.

Two army trucks were parked at the entrance to the town. There were long rows of men facing them. I noticed that each of the men was giving his machete to the soldiers and getting in turn a piece of printed paper.

"What's happening?" I asked the officer who was overseeing the operation.

"We are disarming the peasants of this area," he said. "There are orders to shoot anyone found this afternoon with a machete or without a safe-conduct."

Other soldiers were directing the disarmed peasants to the square.

"And why are you doing that?" I asked, agitated.

The officer shrugged.

"General Calderón will come from San Salvador within a few hours to address them, and he wants all of them to be assembled in the square."

I walked back, pensive, toward the tavern. The measures they were taking seemed severe to me, but they were probably justified under the circumstances. With such a mass of people in the town it was going to be difficult for me to find a place to stay unless I could remain at the tavern. I quickened my steps.

My table was still vacant. There were no soldiers among the numerous clientele, they were all Indians who had come down from the hills. The faint hum of their conversation ceased abruptly when I entered. Their expressions all became harsh and suspicious toward me, making me feel like an intruder. Should I leave? Smile? I sat down at my table with a new bottle of liquor and began my task with the slow rhythm of the good drinker who has a long way to go. An unshaven man kept looking at me over the edge of his empty glass. I gestured to him to join me for a drink, but he shook his head glumly and looked away.

I kept on drinking, my eyes fixed on my table. Little by little the peasants forgot about my being there and again started to talk softly, without altering the expressions on their faces.

The bottle was half empty when I spotted Virgil at the door, looking for me.

"Hello," I greeted him, "when did you get back from Guatemala?"

He waved and came to sit beside me.

"They are keeping you hanging again, eh Frank?"

"It seems so," I replied, "but I still have no broken bones."

"Do you want a drink?"

He declined and ordered a soda.

They didn't allow Virgil to park Edward's car on any of the streets surrounding the plaza. We made our way through the crowd toward the corner where he had left the car. The intersection was blocked by soldiers who wouldn't let us pass.

"Nobody's allowed to leave," a fat sergeant informed us.

"We're going to get our car on the next block," I said. "We have nothing to do with what is happening here."

"I'm carrying out my orders," he replied, unperturbed.

I muttered a few swear words and once more dragged Virgil through the throng, toward the headquarters.

"The captain can't see you now," a soldier told me.

"All we need is a permit to leave the square," I declared.

"There are strict orders that no one leave. The general will be here in a few minutes."

"We're strangers," said Virgil. "The general doesn't care

if we hear what he has to say."

The soldier shrugged and turned to a messenger who was just arriving.

"Let's try another route, Frank," said Virgil, "I'd like to get out of here as quickly as possible."

"Don't worry," I calmed him, "the general is going to give them a tongue-lashing, that's all."

Once more we pushed and shoved our way through the tightly packed square, toward the tavern. Virgil pulled himself up to his full height and told one of the soldiers authoritatively: "My car is in the next block, please let us pass."

The soldier hesitated and seemed to be about to yield when a sergeant approached.

"You know what your orders are," he said, his eyes fixed intently on the soldier. "No one leaves here until the general has finished his speech."

Virgil looked at me, discouraged, and shook his head. I remembered the half-full bottle I had left in the tavern and felt, suddenly, that I was dying of thirst.

"Let's go over into the shade," I said. "The last thing I want is to stand here listening to patriotic speeches."

I cleverly led him toward the tavern, wondering whether I should continue drinking liquor or switch to beer.

"No, Frank," he seemed to read my thoughts, "don't drink anymore."

"That's not fair, Virgil." I looked at him offended. "I have a plan for getting us out of here."

The tavern door was locked. I knocked and the old lady appeared at the window and looked at us with a startled expression.

"Open for me, Granny," I smiled at her, "do it for your best customer."

Another soldier appeared suddenly beside me.

"It's closed," he said, "all the businesses in the square are closed."

I pointed in the direction of the headquarters.

"But my friend," I said, "the captain has just asked me to bring him a cold beer. He assured me that they would let me into the tavern."

The soldier looked at me suspiciously, but I had a white skin and blue eyes. I might be a friend of the general's. With a gesture of irritation he ordered the old lady to let us in.

Satisfied with myself, I sank into a chair.

"Don't you see?" I looked radiantly at Virgil, "isn't this better than cooking our heads in the sun? A large beer for me and a soda for my friend," I hurried to order from the old lady before Virgil could object.

"What's your great plan?" Virgil asked, warily.

"The first phase has been successfully carried out," I assured him as I sipped my beer. "The next step is to wait here until the general comes and begins his speech. While his loyal troops are listening to him in open-mouthed admiration we can leave through the back door, scale the wall onto an unwatched street and sneak away."

Just then we heard the noise of trucks arriving.

"Welcome, General," I said, raising my glass.

Virgil got up and went to the window. I took advantage of his absence to ask the old lady, frantically, for another beer.

"I don't understand what's happening," said Virgil, looking quite worried. "There are two trucks across the street from the church and one at each corner; all the intersections are blocked."

"It's obvious that the general has no confidence in his oratorical skills," I laughed as I refilled my glass.

At that instant the first **ra ta tat** of machine-gun fire rang out.

"My God, Frank!" Virgil cried out, "it's an ambush! They're firing from the trucks."

I jumped up, knocking over my chair. A whirl of anguished screams stifled the noise of the next gun-bursts. The whole square was in violent motion as a mass of white trousers shook like autumn leaves stirred by a gust of wind.

The machine-guns were mounted on the trucks, with officers manning them. While we looked, the mass of peasants in the open space of the square was coming out of its stupor, was trying, gropingly, to find some gap through which to escape. We felt the wave of anguish that extended from those bodies when they realized that there was no possible escape, that they were trapped.

Across the street we saw three or four torsos hoisted on the heads of their comrades. They had been snatched up from the ground and were trying desperately to reach a low roof. One of them made it. He was dragging himself along the tiles when a machine-gun got to him and that was where he ended up, spread-out. His friends were pinned against the wall by the bullets. Before falling to the ground, they seemed to contract, with sudden jerks.

"To the trucks, head for the trucks," someone near to our window shouted. At first only a few moved forward, then a blind and delirious throng hurled itself, convulsively, toward the mouth of the machine-gun at the street corner nearest to us. They jumped over the corpses of the first victims, they slipped on the blood-stained paving stones, they dragged themselves along, wounded. An officer on the other side of the plaza spun his machine-gun around and interposed an invisible wall that stopped them cold, that squashed them against the ground in a nightmare of extravagant gestures, of shrieks suffocated by bubbles of blood, of white rags strewn about on the ground, soaking up blood. In spite of the deadly barricade, a few peasants managed to reach the row of bayonet-wielding soldiers stationed in front of each truck.

The soldiers ran them through there, leaving them to die among screams and convulsions.

"My God! My God!" Virgil's words were a mixture of imprecation and prayer.

I was paralyzed, still unable to believe what my eyes were seeing. The stacks of corpses were forming a tangled mass that protected the trucks. The last group of peasants that tried to hurl itself onto the machine-guns fell torn to pieces on the bodies of their dead or wounded comrades. The screams continued, but in them there was no longer the tone of anger or surprise. They were agonizing screams of pain. Pure pain.

There was a subtle change. The men who were still alive weren't hurling themselves against the trucks anymore. The senseless surging stopped. It seemed as if the Indians had simultaneously clung to the hope that the whole thing was due to a monstrous error and perhaps if they kept quiet and did not move the machine-guns would also be quiet.

Virgil's hands were twitching and pallid on the cross-pieces of the window. We both held our breath, we shared the same hope. But the machine-guns kept on stuttering. The bottles on the shelves were crashing into each other. The machine-guns spoke in short bursts, in businessmen's sentences. They methodically cleaned the gates, the edges of the square, like a scrupulous housewife who sweeps dust from the cracks and corners to put it in a neat pile in the middle of the floor.

Another convulsion occurred in the large many-headed beast that was in its death's agony under the sun, under the black funnel of smoke that Izalco was emitting and that was drifting, boiling, toward the east. The surviving peasants formed a tight group: clawing and scratching they eluded the metallic bees that ricocheted and whined about them, they dragged themselves by their nails toward the centre of the open space, toward the only temporary refuge offered by the still living wall of their comrades. They were all on the ground: kneeling, on their bellies, or wriggling along. The machine-guns continued with their terse, impertinent monologue; each one cutting through the air at a sharp angle of fire so as to avoid the other trucks and soldiers, each one picking out clear chords in the living circle.

The soldiers standing in front of the trucks had no more reason to use their bayonets; they stood frozen, watching the massacre. The old woman had left the window and was wiping up our table automatically, while tears ran along her wrinkles.

All this had happened in less than a minute. Most of the Indians huddled in the middle of the square were alive; some uninjured, others slightly wounded. Even with half a dozen machine-guns it takes time to kill five or six thousand people.

It was at that moment, while it was starting to dawn on me that what was going on in front of my eyes was real, while the impact of horror and monstrosity pounded my solar plexus, it was then, Isabel, that the most incredible, the most unimaginable thing happened. Someone there in the middle of the convulsed square must have shouted out something. I didn't hear it but it must have been something like: "If they are going to kill us then let us die standing up." He probably didn't shout it but only thought it as he was getting up, but his example, or rather, his idea, reached the minds of all the others by telepathy, sensitized as their minds were by the imminence of death.

Three or four of them got up, then twenty, fifty, a hundred. They got up stiffly as if they were hypnotized, as if they had finally remembered something they had memorized many years earlier, in childhood, but which they had later forgotten for a long long time.

Those who could stand up, those who could take a few

steps, formed an erratic, ragged column and they began to move toward the church, toward the smoking mouths of the two hysterical machine-guns that were threatening them from the trucks, opposite the church. A ripple seemed to pass through the head of the column and it broke like a wave on the sand. They were falling, walking, falling. Many of them, all of them fell, squirmed for a while and then became still. Others got up to take their place like sleepwalkers. They walked over corpses and the wounded toward the two trucks.

"No!" Virgil sobbed, "No! No!" and he dashed toward the door. I caught up with him while he was struggling with the key, but with unnatural strength he broke away from me.

"Virgil, don't be an idiot!" I shouted. But it was too late.

It was as if he and I had also learned our roles as children and we were remembering them only now.

Virgil had gone outside, and I?

I went back to the window.

A man and a boy of twelve or thirteen were getting up. The boy was looking at his father, terrorized but obedient.

"Get away from there," the old lady shouted at me.

Virgil walked away from the tavern. He took the boy's other hand. The three of them began to walk toward the church. The old lady came and stood next to me. I followed them with my eyes until they fell.

from CRUMBS
Claudia Lars

Papa Justo, the Indian
lay sown among bullets and curses.
I believe that from his bones
a new corn is sprouting.

from ANECDOTES, CHRONOLOGY, AND
OBITUARY OF BOOTS
Mercedes Durand

He sat down in his chair
after watching
thirty thousand peasants die.
That night he had for supper
herbal soup
boiled pumpkin blossoms
and lemon juice...
He was a theosophist
vegetarian
orientalist
and knew the fine points of witchcraft.
He put water
to settle in the sun
in pretty painted bottles
and wouldn't stand for
the killing
of an ant
a mosquito
or a spider.
He never looked anyone in the eye.
He worshipped Hitler
and Mussolini.

THE REPUBLIC OF POWER
Alfonso Hernández

Every year the dictator makes a speech to the multitudes
from his pragmatic throne "Peace Love Justice"
(as if history were an expedient of his base passions).
The dictator makes his speech,
the promise of new schools; a plan for putting an end to
hunger, illiteracy, and many other things;
and also an agrarian reform for those who have
rosy dreams, who view
life as benign.
Every year, as I have said,
with high honours he raises his funereal hand to make
the sign of the cross
over hundreds of sickening corpses...

from *MYTHOLOGY OF CUZCATLÁN*
Miguel Angel Espino

The present of a people is the result of its past.

from *CHILDHOOD STORIES*
José María Cuéllar

I was born in 1942 if for some reason my mother
has not lost her memory.
At age five I learned that thirty thousand peasants died
because they were hungry.
It was then I realized that in my country to be hungry
                                              is a crime.
The village where I was born has a bad history.
They say that around 1798,
an administrator from the Central Province
had these lands peopled by Spaniards
who vaunting their lineage
mounted Indian women and more Indian women as if
                          going through an endless train.
One of these descendants of the Cid
surprised one of my great-great-grandmothers bathing
                                      in the Copinolapa River
and with the brusqueness of a centaur,
made her the cornerstone of my family.

from *RIDING HOOD IN THE RED ZONE*
Manlio Argueta

"Mamma dear. A prayer for everyone. Mamma you are so full of grace. Vendor in the markets. Mamma buying bottles from door to door. Mamma whore. Mamma who roams the streets with policemen on her trail. Mamma, how are you? Mamma like all soulful things. Mamma coffee picker. Who gathers flowers by the roadside to put them in tin vases. Mamma dependable. Mamma in sickness. Mamma virgin maria mother of god. Sacred name. Mamma lighter of candles to the holy child of Atocha and beautiful San Antonio. Mamma in those dark streets. Vendor of fermented corn drinks and pineapple tarts. Mamma parading through the streets with newspaper hats to shield himself from the sun and a bag of fried beans and little tortillas in case the parade lasts a long time. Mamma of the Union of Slum Dwellers. Mamma barefooted. Mamma ready to run outside in case there are bullets. Mamma diligent. Cotton picker under the stinging sun of the coast. Where are you? One fine day god, when you love me a little, I will build a house where we both will live. Hello mamma Bad mother. Lullaby little child. Your day, day dying of hunger. Mamma pleading to them free my son, he hasn't done anything, shut up you old whore. Mamma I'm going to be back late. Mamma in the morgue. Mamma mine. Mamma searching among the dead. Mamma virgin, alone. Mamma saying it is the body that trembles and not the spirit. Mamma saying return my son's body. Mamma man, grandmother, grandfather, mamma, mamma. Your mother. Good morning, mamma."

from *ONE DAY OF LIFE*
Manlio Argueta

As they say:

You've got to realize that all these women are a bunch
of whores. To be a woman is to have been born a whore,
while men are divided into two classes: gays, and we
macho men, who wear this uniform; and from among
the macho men should be chosen the most most most
macho: those of the Special Forces, those of us who have
gone through school with the Chinese karate experts and
the white psychologists. Those of us who grow strong on
mashed potatoes. We can't be gentle with our enemies,
we must be iron-willed, resolute; we aren't like the Nica-
raguans, who only know how to kill but who do not show
proper regard for their status in their dealings with the
civilian population, they eat with them, they accept invita-
tions from them, and that is an indication of a lack of self-
respect; to be sociable is to be sissy. Nor are we like the
Hondurans who admit into their ranks any riffraff what-
soever and for this reason they are always talking there
about divisions among the ranks, about all kinds of nationalism. We are different, we are compact. We are united
to the death and we don't go around building up the confidence of the civilians. God forbid, because if you give an
ordinary Salvadorean an inch he takes a mile; if you laugh

along with him he's sure you're a whore or a fruit. So you can't go playing the ass with civilians. You fall asleep and, like shrimp, the current sweeps you away. Besides, there's something else, the Salvadorean has a predilection for communism, ever since 1932.

So how are we going to be nationalist, if nationalism says that we're all equal? And the truth is that we're not equal to the other people, that can't exist here, for how are we going to be equal to a civilian population that is strongly attracted to communism? We prefer the foreign element because foreigners don't come here to screw us, they almost always come to do good. At the same time the native, only because he's a native, thinks he has the right to shit on us. That's why we cut off his water; and if killing is called for, we kill the Salvadorean, because the Salvadorean has one main characteristic: that of being a son of a bitch. It isn't that I want to give my people hell, it's just the plain truth and Christ died for the truth. The day the ordinary civilian population gets hold of the presidency of the republic, forget it, they will hang us all by the balls. And it isn't necessary for the American from the Special Forces to emphasize this point, we already know it. Because the important thing, the American tells us, isn't that you're here for the pay, or for the good food you're getting, but out of conviction, you're God's soldiers, the saviours of this country that's going to hell now and in love with communism.

Look how in 1932 the communists hadn't even triumphed before they started abusing people, rich people, for these people really hate the rich; we were born with envy inside us, we can't stand the sight of contentment in other people's eyes because right away we start thinking of how to give them hell. And we're here precisely to prevent envy, to exterminate it by force of bullets, decisiveness and firmness. We're preparing ourselves more and more, because communism is coming. Our foreign teachers don't leave us alone for a single minute. They say they're ready to die with us for liberty and democracy, to eliminate all vestiges of nationalism. I agree totally: the race has to be exterminated by fire. All this nastiness will end when we're all united in Christ, when we embrace Christ, when we do away with the communist priests. You won't believe it, but we have classes in religion, in the true, the other religion, the one that comes to us from up there. The classes allow us to choose among the Latter-Day-Saints, the Mormons, or the Jehovah's Witnesses, religions which bring light and hope for the eternal happiness of mankind.

Therefore we can't go around respecting those relationships such as brothers and sisters, uncles and aunts, cousins and even parents. If they choose the path of darkness, it's their business, let each one look out for his own skin. To hell with them if they want to act stupid. And if they want bullets then let them play the fool, because they will get heaps of them. We can't go around being lenient, much less sentimental.

As for the women, the older they are the more whorish. That is the truth. It is all clear even though some doubt it, especially with regard to their mothers, but the American explains: that is to say, all those who at a given moment oppose or are an obstacle to the country's security. Well, maybe there are exceptions, but very few. For example, I believe that my mamma is not a whore and she will never be one since I'm going to help her so that she will not come to sympathize with the enemy camp. Our teachers tell us: you have to help your families see the light. Of course, we can't go around wasting time with people, for just because people are relatives that doesn't mean that they aren't brutes. I myself have some cousins who are getting themselves involved in some stupid things. I've already warned them, indirectly, since I don't want to have any problems with my parents, who are still in the dark, though I'm not going to tell the instructors since they wouldn't understand. It's not because I'm afraid.

Then again my sisters, they are something else. They, like all women, have been looking for husbands since they were little girls, at fifteen they were already looking for company. That's why there's so much poverty in this country, because since the women are whores they don't wait long before they have children. The women are most to blame for the existence of so much poverty. Look, we're more than four million in a little tiny space and so they want the lands to be divided up. Just imagine how much each person would get; a piece hardly big enough to stand on. I don't say they're stupid. There wouldn't be enough even for a grave. For certainly if the land is going to be divided up, it has to be done fairly and each person should get an equal share, if not it would be better for them to stop walking around talking crap.

As for our sisters, when the men get bored with them, you see them coming back to their parents so that they can take care of the children which they're now stuck with. I tell you, they're out-and-out whores. That's why when we have some tranquillity here again, that is, when we don't have so many agitators because we will have exterminated all of them, our task isn't going to end but is going to take another form: for example, to carry out family planning campaigns, to set up strict birth-control programs. That will be our future mission. The fatherland will be great when it only has the children necessary for loving it, respecting it, and dying for it.

There'll be a lot of work for us too with regard to religion, convincing people to embrace Christ. We'll have to put a stop to all the foolishness. For in the year 1990 when He comes to earth, as it is prophesied, only those of us who are in Christ will be saved. Because He's going to come to punish everyone, except His own.

In addition, possibly all this will happen sooner; the date of His coming may change. So our mission must be carried out as quickly as possible, and we must act with boldness, decisiveness, and firmness.

No leniency, whether you're my friend or buddy, or my brother. That's all foolishness. We're together or we're not together. The rest isn't worth a prick.

I'm really not such a brute. The class I like most is the psychology class. I'm a little weak in karate. But that's how it goes.

I was saved by the fact that I finished the sixth grade and I was very good at social sciences, so I was chosen for the Special Forces.

That's how I've moved up. My family is poor. My brothers couldn't study, they preferred to work rather than to study, and when they turned seven they went off with my father to pick coffee, cotton, and cocoa. That is the cut-off age: you either go to school or to work. I began to work when I was seven, but later they sent me to school and the teacher said I was bright and they should send me even if it were irregularly. It was a struggle for me to get through grade six. But look at me. Here I am. No one can snatch away from me what has cost me so much.

And then I went to San Salvador and found success. Well, my sisters also came to San Salvador, but since they became weighed down with children they went to unload them on my parents and came back, but you can imagine how. What's more, they say that two of them were seen along Independence Avenue, which is where the bad women live. They are selling their bodies, it seems. Once I used to be a little ashamed to say it; now I'm not because the American teacher has told us that this is the good thing about democracy: everyone can do as he or she pleases, there is individual freedom.

It has its injustices, of course. We should be honest in recognizing that. But democracy is like that. The busi-

ness of everybody being equal is pure rubbish. The world
has progressed precisely because we're not equal. Just
imagine, how am I going to be equal to the Chinaman?
He is a karate expert, I'm not. How is my sister going to
be equal to those girls who ride in horse-shows? It would
be idiotic. God made us equal to everyone else but each
one with his differences.

I remember when I used to go with the whole family
to pick cotton. We took along even the youngest girl who
had just turned seven; with our sun-hats and a paper
bag of food and rags for sleeping on. All of us off to pick
while the foreman took down the names. The names of
the little ones weren't taken because to have your name
taken means to have a right to tortillas and beans and
they weren't going to give them to everyone, only to the
adults. But we carried our salt so that we could fill ourselves up with salted tortillas. And water. We carried water in calabashes.

And no one died of hunger. Well, two of my brothers
died but that was due to my mother's carelessness. When
their diarrhoea started she stood by doing nothing and
they died of a collapsed brain.

Almost all the children in the countryside die of a collapsed brain. Due perhaps to our own ignorance we
stand around and then we go to the drugstore when it is
too late. And since there are no doctors...

But whores, there sure are whores.

And the instructor tells us: "You ought to respect that
uniform."

"You ought to respect it even when you are in bed with
a woman." And then a smart-aleck blurts out to the
American:

"When you are in bed with a woman you don't have a
uniform on or anything." And what else could he ask for?
Snickers from everybody. Then the American grabbed a
duster that had a wooden base and threw it, hitting the

smart-aleck in his face. Tremendous swelling around his eye. And off to the infirmary.

So it's not just a question of horsing around. This uniform is my life. It has made me sweat blood.

The other night someone cracked a loud fart. The keen ears of the American who was writing at the other side of the hut heard the blessed fart. We were all quiet when the American opened the door and the light streamed in on us. He didn't say anything and went outside into the garden. Our barracks is like a shed, it has no walls, only a roof, so that we can accustom ourselves to the surroundings. Well, guess what he was doing: he connected a hose to the tap and bathed us all. That night we couldn't sleep because the cold and the wet sheets and the mattresses froze the very shit inside us.

He told us:

"Take that for playing the fool." You see, then, what I'm telling you.

The shit. Even though I respect him a lot. And at that I'm not telling you anything about the training because it's a secret.

So this uniform that you see me wearing so proudly isn't a simple thing.

Then they go about saying that we don't have to work to earn a living, that we only hunt down people. That is said by those who don't know a damned thing. Or by enemies of the fatherland. Because no honest person is going to go around saying things that he doesn't know.

from CRUMBS
Claudia Lars

I saw the masked men
throwing truth into a well.
When I began to weep for it
I found it everywhere.

from *CASIANGA*
Roberto Monterroza

people of the orphanhood of the latrine perjurer
people like he-goats
people of the negative street
street of blows to the head and saliva
street without understanding
street of the kick in the pants
street of the heritage that divides in order to conquer
street of the benzedrine lunatic
lunatic loved by the girls
lunatic with a gun on his shoulder
lunatic in shorts dancing the rumba
lunatic of the railway station
people who fasten the lock
people of stunted vision
people of the latrine
people of the empty cartridge who don't matter.

THE MURDER OF THE POLO CHAMPION
Alfonso Quijada Urías

They killed the polo champion.
The man of a thousand suits,
the same one who had mansions
and yachts
and rich and pretty women almost the world over.
They shot him dead
and threw him, hands tied,
into a ditch.
They killed him because he abandoned his suits,
his horses and polo,
his yachts and mansions,
and above all because he began to walk
like a poor man among the poor.

MY FRIENDS
Carlos Aragón

(In semi-syncopated flow)

Where are they? Where are they?
Where are my old friends?
Those from our little school
and those from the university...

Juan studied medicine
he enjoyed conversation
now he is somewhere in Europe
he fled from the social year...

Cecilia studied law
intent on changing things
now she has her lawyer's office
and likes champagne...

Where are they? Where are they?
Where are my old friends?
Those from our little school
and those from the university...

Pedro is an economist
he has given up music
he has sold his piano
and now only knows how to add...

Antonio was a humanist
he used to like to draw
now he is a publicist
who is very quick to collect...

Where are they? Where are they?
Where are my old friends?
Those from our little school
and those from the university...

There was one we didn't know
who liked the sea
—his name was Felipe—
he had clear and tranquil eyes
and his walk was serene...

Today the guns roared,
the sea has started to cry,
they killed the one we didn't know,
the struggle has now begun...

Where are they? Where are they?
Where are my old friends?
Those from our little school
and those from the university...

from *Sniping*
José María Méndez

I had the idea that a National Budget was something serious, that it couldn't serve as a vehicle for telling jokes. I have changed my mind. I read in the Budget prepared for this year, in the chapter devoted to the National University, the following:

Subvention to form the endowment of the University (in keeping with the Political Constitution and Article 26 of the Organic Law) for the construction of the new University Campus .... ¢ 1.00.

In the actual Budget one colón, one miserable colón, is earmarked to form the endowment for the construction of the University Campus. Doesn't this seem to you to be a budgetary joke?

That colón, someone has explained to me, is a symbolic colón. It is destined not to be spent. When an entry that should appear in the budget is not filled in with the adequate sum, that system of writing in one colón is used. Thus, he explains further, the entry exists as an accountable item even though it doesn't exist in reality.

I don't understand this! I definitely don't understand it. As far as I am concerned, what they have done is to allocate to so important an objective as the building of a University Campus a ridiculous sum: one colón. And I say: if that is the amount allocated, it should be spent. How?

I would spend it like this:

Lime .... ¢ 0.25
Sand .... ¢ 0.25
Saltpetre .... ¢ 0.25
Gunpowder .... ¢ 0.25

With these purchases (lime, sand, saltpetre, and gunpowder) I would prepare a mixture and make those who prepared the Budget swallow it.

A SONG
Paco Barrios

The wild cat sharpens its claws,
the sparrowhawk its talons,
the feet of the poor Indian
are more beautiful than boots.

Long live freedom
and those who work for the people,
those who die each day
in the cause of truth.

The lamp is not to be kept
under a bushel
light should illuminate
all humanity.

The wild cat sharpens its claws,
the sparrowhawk its talons,
the feet of the poor Indian
are more beautiful than boots.

Long live freedom
and the workers for the people
those who die each day
in the cause of truth.

In Memory of Comrade Juan Castro
Sonia Civallero

The flower of San Andrés bursts open
while you,
Mario González,
Alexander López,
Juan Castro,
founder of the inn "La Bolsa"
coffee picker in Cantarrana
conductor on route 7
or seller of saints,
left your hunger hanging behind the door,
embraced the rosary of grenades,
greased your weapon,
put on firmly the cap woven by your grandmother,
tied on your handkerchief to cover your face,
from your cheekbone to the tip of your chin
and in a frenetic attack you tore up the stars
you ignited the minute of fury
you knew of unnoticed noises
you savoured the delights of battle.
And,
finally,
your nineteen Januarys
died in the middle of a street...

Wounded by machine-guns
the innocent one lay forgetting his fright
in his modest coffin.
Contemplating him I lost forever
my seventy-year-old infancy.

from *ORGANIZED POETRY*
Róger Lindo

Hidden away from my great weaknesses
I trace for myself the daily
anomalous pattern of combat
clearly conscious of my role but bothered somewhat
by the condition of not wanting to tell it all

I have invaded the scene with surprising grace
I have felt the little antennae of bullets probing me
            mistakenly
I have felt the great confusion I swear
and here I am
unbendable

I have also taken myself by the hand
to corners where no justifications serve
after proposing such actions to myself
not without a certain efficient and pedagogic malevolence

The sole sadness now is the effect of so many lights
or the dizziness among so many faces

I am a man
half-accustomed to dehumanizing himself
who recovered by dint of an effort
akin to desperation
and began to touch the world beneficially

But everything can be put right
and in that context
you are one of the best possibilities
for me who as I was saying
is accustomed to confusion
mistaken for a state of excessive lucidity

I almost shun you not knowing if I understand
how to accept chief responsibility
for some basic task
perhaps because in your smile I reconstruct
as in a fragile model
the anxious and profound part of this commitment:
It might be said that you are the reflection
poetically corrected and enlarged
of this so clear alternative
to which I now dedicate myself

Testimony
Alfonso Hernández

We were together at the federation,
we were ten young people, and
each one was talking about his experiences...
nobody was thinking about death,
death of a thousand faces.
But the fateful hour came
and tens of policemen from the "Death Squad"
        burst into the room.
Shots rang out immediately,
two comrades fell murdered.
We were unarmed,
we had only a notebook.
We were bound, face down, and put into a Ford.

"So you are the ones who are going around saying
        Fatherland or Death!"
"Well start praying because you have come up with
death!"

We were eight:
on the way to Los Naranjos they made six get out, and
tying them by the ankles, they bound them with strong
        ropes to a tree trunk;

their hands were tied to the bumper of the truck,
then they moved the truck off suddenly
and we heard the screams.

The six pairs of hands, bloodied, hung from the bumper
          of the truck, and
the policemen were enjoying themselves.
Then they finished them off.
Only Raul and I were left...
After a few kilometres they made us get out
with our hands still tied.
Raul whispered.
          "We are facing death
          and we must run any risk
          to escape..."

Those were his last words, and
rapidly we dashed toward a precipice
but Raul slipped and was riddled with bullets;
he fell from branch to branch to the bottom.
I managed to steal away through the bushes.

THE HIGHWAYS THAT LED SOUTH
Gabriela Yanes

The highways that led south
are now filled with corpses
the coffee plantations radiate a strange freshness
at night the dead
are absorbed through the pores of the earth
eventually they bloom as red coffee trees

(a cynical blackbird
eats up the ripe guavas)

the earth is slowly tiring

of children sweet as figs

from OUR FATHER
Alfonso Quijada Urías

There was a humble little priest in my village,
a little priest who would sit down with the peasants,
the workers and the students; with everyone but the rich.
A little man who decorated his cassock with happy
        woven fabrics from Chichicastenango
(because happiness is the most revolutionary thing
        there is),
and he spoke with the words of the poor and the
        persecuted
and his church was filled with songs and peasant guitars.
And the powerful gentlemen, the owners of the
        country's wealth,
did not enter through its doors
"because it is not right that a few should store it all up
        in their coffers."
And his words were clear and neither the bankers
nor their lawyer-gangsters
nor even the imperialists to whom he wrote a letter
saying:
"NO EMPIRE HAS A RIGHT TO COME TO INFLUENCE
THE WAY OF LIFE OF OUR PEOPLE"
could withstand him.

And the little man who was an archbishop, but
      above all a MAN
became the target of their insults
because in his church there congregated those hungry
      for bread
and for justice
and the press refused to print his homilies
and opened up instead their publishing houses and
      paid media
to insult him
and the rulers of the republic with their managers
      and their bishops
and priests like rats and buzzards began to hang
      about his room
where he wrote his homilies until dawn.
And since his voice, which was "the voice of the
      voiceless," would not be silent
despite the threats,
the bankers and their managers and the managers
      with their bishops
and priests as gloomy as buzzards paid an assassin
and the sure and expert hand hired in Miami
wiped him out with one single shot to the heart.

from THE NIGHT OF THE PURSUED
Salomón Rivera

The night of the pursued
is nothing but the encounter
with an inescapable truth.
Along with that truth — as certain as life and death —
a people's destiny orients their actions
like an insistent sound that comes demolishing
      everything.

REASONS FOR SURPRISE
José Luis Valle

Threats. Blows upon blows.
Shadows and fears. Instabilities.
Repression and exile. One dictator after another.
From each dark spot: two stones
At each street corner: three or more opportunists
In each cafeteria: four or more informers
I am still surviving. And that surprises me.

from A WAY OF DYING
Reyes Gilberto Arévalo

At any moment everything will be definitive
you won't have time to bequeath to your wife
the poverty of your memories
you will surely watch your words
and the children will be afraid to come near
Dripping from your body
will be the love of those times when you would
      reach home
to put your hand on your children's shoulders
People will want to know your name
and when they find you
more than one will say an "Our father"
and if you are lucky three Ave Marías
to illuminate your silence
they will light four cheap candles for you
and as they do routinely tie handkerchiefs over their faces
Thus sadness will make you solemn
and the wind will make you rigid
while the judge arrives dutifully
to lie about the cause of your death

from *WITHOUT CEREMONY*
Roberto Quesada

I
Pathologist for this area,
request permission
of the trial judge
of the ant-hill on the patio
to carry out an autopsy
on ant number 170177:

SUSPECTED VICTIM OF POISONING

But no,
she was captured by the big-headed ants
of the patio of the house next door
and interrogated on the park lawn

SHE WAS INTERROGATED
TORTURED
AND MURDERED ON THE PARK LAWN

from *THE INFINITE HEADS*
Eduardo Sancho Castañeda

They detained my friend in his Sunday clothes
accused him of dynamiting stars
kissing sleeping children
playing with a little box of centipedes
having an angelic smile

afterwards they wasted him in the sea
with a rope to the neck of his good disposition.

from MAKING MY SONG
Miguel Huezo Mixco

With the soft
or hard things
the day offers me
on the tip of its brilliant
razor-like tongue
my song must begin to take form.

That pincushion stuck like a thorn
to the seat of pain,
where love is transformed
and combat exposes in hatred
a rose,
must be the site of my song,
where life surrenders itself
unreservedly
to life.

from THE POET AND HIS WIFE
Julio Iraheta Santos

If I could only open a small shop
and hang out a sign saying:
POEMS MADE AND REPAIRED HERE.

But people would pass by indifferently...

from NOW THAT YOU ARE NAKED
Nelson Brizuela

Some day you will reach the conclusion
that you have to take life
by the horns, that now that they have closed
the door in your face you shouldn't ring the bell
and that it is more than just
to seize justice by the scruff of the neck
till you make it vomit from remorse.

Some day you will realize
that suicide is not a friend,
much less an intelligent exit
for a good boy like you,
who believes in a new world order,
for a boy who now
is a monster with divine voice,
toothless and sad,
who sings alone when
they have turned the lights out on humanity
and they squeeze the testicles of its history.

from LIFE, PASSION, AND DEATH OF THE ANTI-MAN
Pedro Geoffroy Rivas

We lived on a false premise,
riding atop a loathsome world of lies,
perched upon illusory stages,
making castles in the air,
blowing vain soap bubbles,
shattering dreams.

And in the meantime,
others kneaded our bread with blood,
others made our haughty bed with painful hands
and sweated to provide for us the milk their children
        never had.

Oh, my former life with no greater objective
than to sing, sing, sing,
like some blessed old-maid's canary.
Oh, my twenty-five years wasted in the streets.
Twenty-five rotten years that did nothing for anyone.

Poor little poet that I was, bourgeois and good.
Spermatozoid of a lawyer with his client.
Caterpillar of a landowner with huge coffee plantations
        and thousands of slaves.
Embryo of a feudal lord, violator of young women and
        dark peasant slave girls.

And I have died in full bloom of my years and half-way
        through the loud laughter of life,
when I represented a promise for several families
and a clear hope for two or three countries.

Theory for Dying in Silence
Ricardo Castrorrivas

To Francisco Gavidia

(hypocritical office rats cork men always afloat even though the successive governments sink always looking for a chance to have your photograph come out in the newspapers and show it proudly in the neighbourhood look at my eyes and see that I despise you for being servile mediocre ignorant you who never learned to say no why don't you go away and leave me in peace take your slobber and your flattery where they are well paid I want nothing from you multiple men in the fraudulent elections paid hacks when it comes to justifying a coup d'etat potential deviates lying racketeers get lost understand the look in my eyes I want nothing why do you come contrite today putting on airs saying that the supreme government recognizes the meritorious work of a great man and bring medicines medical books the keys to an Institute of Housing house and also the reporters the photographers the ladies of the Good Heart and I want nothing look into my eyes look at me you think I am happy yes I hear you that vicious old lady says she discerns in my face gratitude and it is not true what I really want is for you to go away study my eyes carefully I want nothing why should I what I want is tranquillity to hell with the glory the medals the esteem the parchments the prizes the publication of my complete works the posthumous homages the lifetime pension for my children to hell with all that I tell you everything with these eyes that weep from pure rage and you are saying that I weep from gratitude you swine what I would really be grateful for is for you all to go away leave me silence leave me silence)

from I STAND FIRM HERE
Jaime Suárez Quemain

I know that the death of a poet
doesn't get the admiration of the idiots
who wait to see him good and dead to exclaim:
"What a fine poet he was"
"these boys of today
ought to follow his example."
As if in the long run
it mattered a crumb
to be the subject of small talk
among people who have never come near
to probe into my sacrosanct miasma.

Arrivistes of verse,
dedicated smokers of that stinking opium:
poetry
either shields its testicles
and fights in the streets with clean verse
or it limits itself to being a bedroom toy
for frustrated lovers.

from NOW THAT YOU ARE NAKED
Nelson Brizuela

These times have scarred poetry,
have stricken it with death
and it can no longer be an act of peace
emerging from a common perspective. Today it is written
with the need to bring to light
this way of looking at the world with wide open eyes,
this passing of the tongue
over people's wounds,
this wanting to stop the blood
that runs and runs
like an eternally open tap.

from *THE INFINITE HEADS*
Eduardo Sancho Castañeda

some poets build a cathedral of words
so that strange beings might enter and sit in
armchairs to await the magic touch of superstitions

others await their mausoleum date with a heroic
     little medal
some see in poetry a show-jumping contest of noses
and they have godlike mucus
others climb down from the cross in dinner jackets

others get buried in grass mats.

from As a Declaration of Principles
Roque Dalton

Regardless of his quality, his performance, his excellence, his creative capacity, his success, for the bourgeoisie the poet can only be:

SERVANT
CLOWN
OR
ENEMY

The clown is an "independent" servant who handles nothing better than the limits of his own "freedom" and who one day comes to hurl in people's faces the view that the bourgeoisie "certainly has sensitivity." Strictly speaking the servant can wear the uniform of a lackey or a minister or a cultural representative working abroad, and even silk pyjamas for going to bed with his most distinguished lady.

The enemy poet is above all the enemy poet. He demands payment not in flattery nor in dollars but in persecutions, prisons, bullets. And he will not only lack uniforms, monkey suits and evening dress, but each day he will find himself with fewer things until all he has left is a couple of shirts that are patched but clear like true poetry.

A Note from a Salvadorean Newspaper
La Prensa Gráfica

TRAGIC ASSASSINATION OF TWO NEWSPAPER REPORTERS

Completely disfigured by machete and firearm wounds to their heads and different parts of their bodies, the corpses of the journalist Jaime Suárez Quemain, 30-year-old editor of the daily La Crónica, and of the photographer César Najarro, 24 years old, who until a month ago worked for this same newspaper, were found on Saturday at 7:30 a.m. in the area known as "Lomas de San Francisco."

As reported in yesterday's edition of La Prensa Gráfica, in the section entitled "Last Night's Events," both were kidnapped at about 6 p.m. on Friday by four men heavily armed with machine-guns, who oblig— See p.49

TRAGIC...

—Continued from p.2
ed them to get into an unidentified taxi and carried them off to an unknown destination. It is reported that the journalist Suárez Quemain and the photographer Najarro were together with several friends having a drink when the unidentified men appeared and took them away forcibly, threatening them. The names of the friends who were with them are not known.

Corpses found

At dawn on Saturday, at about 7 a.m., the Justice of the Peace of Antiguo Cuscatlán was informed of the discovery of two corpses of two good-looking young men in "Lomas de San Francisco." When he went to the site of the discovery he found many people already there, among them relatives of the two deceased, who had been alerted by other information media that were reporting the news. From these people he managed to establish that the corpses belonged to the journalist and writer Suárez Quemain and the photographer Najarro, kidnapped on the previous day from the restaurant "Beautiful Naples."

Completely disfigured

Both corpses had completely disfigured faces and presented a truly macabre sight. The face of the journalist and writer Jaime Suárez Quemain, according to the pathologist's report, showed the following wounds: a machete blow that virtually beheaded him from the front of his neck and through his right cheek, some 30 centimetres long; another wound in the forehead and adjoining area, which damaged his ear, cheekbone and left cheek; another razor-like wound in his umbilical area that went deep into his abdomen; a machete chop on the outer part of his left elbow, some 10 centimetres long; another one 15 centimetres long on his left knuckle that extended to a part of his arm. On the lower part of his left leg were three sharp machete wounds and on his right leg a deep wound of about 6 centimetres in length. Finally, on his head, there was a wound on the right side and another on his right temple, both of them machete wounds, deep, and some 30 centimetres long, which practically split his head in two, in addition to a wound caused by a bullet that possibly entered his mouth and had no exit wound. His corpse also showed signs of torture, all of which indicates that before he was killed he was physically abused, as was César Najarro.

BIOGRAPHICAL DATA

According to statements made by his relatives, the journalist and writer Suárez Quemain was the son of the late champion boxer Alex Suárez, and *doña* Carlota Quemain, the boxer's widow. Suárez Quemain had been working for two years for the newspaper *La Crónica* as editor-in-chief. From a very early age he showed a flair for writing and practised both prose and poetry...

from CONCERNING OUR POETIC ETHICS
Roque Dalton

We are not, then, comfortable and unpunished
         nameless people:
we are openly against the enemy
and we ride very close to him, on the same track.

And to the system and the men
we attack through our poetry
with our lives we give the chance to come around,
day after day.

from THE WAR WE ARE GOING TO WIN
Manuel Sorto

The impeccable
savage
renewing
metaphor
of the Salvadorean poem
is protected in the boy
who prepares for the war

The best internal rhythm
of our poem
is measured
in the effectiveness of the attack
in the appropriateness of the withdrawal

from *ONE DAY OF LIFE*
Manlio Argueta

As they say:

You see, we'd never eaten with fork or spoon (what luxury!), they gleam like they were made of silver or gold. Well, I'd only used gourd spoons, those that we make ourselves, that we use to eat hot fermented corn-drink, and that should be scraped clean every now and then with a piece of glass. The bad thing about those silver spoons is that they burn your mouth, while the gourd spoon doesn't have that defect; you drink the hot corn-drink and nothing happens.

We'd certainly never eaten on tablecloths, like the cloths used for wrapping tortillas but much bigger and with coloured patterns around the edges; and the material is not coarse cotton but something like silk, very fine, you wouldn't believe, like velvet or dove's feathers. And don't talk about the chairs. Well, it's all a piece of paradise. What more could we ask for?

And even if it's true that the instructor, a great big American who really knows his stuff, treats us badly, all in all I wouldn't change my life for any other, so help me. We eat meat everyday. At first, since I wasn't used to it, it caused me trouble, it hurt my stomach. What's more, we don't even eat tortillas and this is something else that at first we have to get accustomed to, since they only serve us bread, smeared with something called margarine or garlic butter; but why am I telling you this, since I know that it's all Greek to you? The other instructor, a Chinaman who doesn't speak Spanish, only gibberish, tells us: You live like princes, if you want to know. You can hardly understand him: "Lib plince, know, know." We want to laugh because his tongue gets all twisted, but we all keep very quiet because God help us if we clash with the Chinaman. He's a good teacher.

Consider, for example, the mashed potato. I didn't know a damn thing about it before, but I'm going to explain it to you. It's something like corn dough, but made with potato, mashed potato dough if you can believe it; at first it's disgusting, difficult to swallow because it's insipid, and they put some little branches of parsley on top of it. But after a time, well, it's a dish for the gods. As the Chinaman says: "Ditch got." I would have liked to bring you a little bit of it for you to taste, but since they search everybody when they leave the base, I wouldn't want them to find mashed potato in my bag. I don't even know why they sometimes call it purée. Look, let me be frank with you, and excuse my language: purée looks like shit except that it has the smell of semen. But we have to force ourselves to eat it. And then it's a matter of getting used to it. They say that the dish was invented in France. I don't know. People in those countries are so inventive.

In the morning, orange juice and a milk they call yogurt. Well the juice is alright; but the yogurt, what a whore, pardon the expression. But let me explain it to you: if mashed potatoes have the smell of semen, yogurt is almost semen itself. And we must swallow it like we swallow worm medicine. At first I would slyly hold my nose to make it go down well, now all I have to do is keep thinking that it's good for me and it goes down without any trouble — like knocking back a shot of rum — in two or three mouthfuls and without tasting it unless you want to vomit; then you are punished for sure. One time one of the guys vomited, and why did the poor man do it? The director told us: "You are a bunch of silly asses. I don't want to see or even hear about any more of that kind of stupidness, remember that." So what can we do? Otherwise, we live like princes.

We should eat well, the American tells us, so we'll be able to defend the country well. In exchange for those pleasures we can't fail our people. We have to be ready to defend the fatherland from its enemies even at the sacrifice of our own brothers; and needless to say, even of our mothers. This may seem exaggerated to you, but the western world is in danger and we know that the greatest danger facing the western world is what they call "the people." The teacher shouts at us: "Who is our worst enemy?" And we answer shouting: "The people." And something like: "Who is the worst enemy of democracy?" And we all answer: "The people." "Louder," he tells us. And we shout at the top of our voices: "The people-the people-the people." I am telling you this in confidence, of course. They call us the Special Forces.

They're instilling all that into us. And it's true, for if it weren't true they wouldn't be lavishing so much on us, giving us so many luxuries. Look, even the cheese is different, the cheese we eat is red on the outside and yellow on the inside, it looks like a jewel. Tell me, when in my whoring and Catholic life did I ever dream of such great deals? No, not everybody gets this, only the Special Forces. All our instructors are foreigners, except for the director, but he's not around much; only once in a while he comes to ask how our discipline is going, how our formation is going. And we all have to reply: "Fine, for the fatherland, Chief."

I'm telling you all this in confidence, be careful not to tell anybody.

And we have instructors in things that you wouldn't dream of; for example, arts; yes, that's what it's called, martial arts, the Chinaman teaches it, even how to gouge out an eye with your thumb. And there is another class called psychology, that is, how you can make the people suffer by using only words; because, as you know, it isn't always necessary to resort to physical force; quite often there are people who understand just words. This science of psychology has something to do with electrical apparatuses.

Only by being tough can we save democracy from danger. But be very careful not to leak a word of this, buddy, as you know a drunkard can't be believed. And then I'd say that you invited me for drinks only to pry things out of me. No, don't be afraid, let's have a drink. I'm inviting you now, buddy, don't walk out on me. And don't go to sleep on me either, because you know that when you are defenceless anything can happen to you.

The American says that the people's soul has been poisoned. They have been brainwashed. This is something scientific, but in this part of the world, being underdeveloped countries, we don't understand what it means. It isn't that we're stupid but we're a country of illiterates, or as they say, backward people, because we were born good-for-nothing. We had the bad luck to be conquered by Spaniards who were nothing but great boozers, while up there in the north, it was the English, who are great workers, who arrived. Besides, the English wiped out the Indians while the Spaniards didn't. That was the great mistake. Because, you know, and it isn't for wanting to speak badly about people's race, but we Indians are lazy, we want everything to fall to us from the sky. We have no drive. Take me, for example, if I hadn't had the courage to leave for the city I'd be like you, no offence meant my friend, but I'd be living from hand to mouth on all this crap, since this stuff that you eat can't be called food. You see, in the United States for example, corn is used only to feed pigs and horses, and to think that we here are satisfied with eating only tortilla and salt.

As I was telling you, it's a case of pure bad luck, even with religion everything has turned out badly for us. While up there, in the United States, the true Christ came with those modern churches they call Jehovah's Witnesses and Mormons, with big white elegantly dressed parsons who both spread the word of God and master sciences like psychology and karate, the Spaniards brought us syphilis and the Catholic religion which is poisoned by pure communism. Of course, they say, the Spaniards didn't go around killing Indians, on the contrary they slept with Indian women and in that way our race came about, but look at our colour, I don't need to tell you that if we were to go to the United States they would take us for blacks and we couldn't enter hotels or buses for whites. What's more they would treat you worse than blacks since they say that even though their colour condemns them the blacks are still considered to be Americans, while we latinos are neither liquor nor lemonade, with this screwed-up colour. It would surely have been better for us to be Indians or whites, without this half-and-half business. It's necessary to define yourself, my friend. But the Spaniards gave us a raw deal even in religion, as I was telling you, since it turns out now that the priests have become worse than the civilians, and we have to see that they're checked, even perhaps by smashing the most abusive ones. You already saw what we did with those we've had to get rid of. The worst thing is that it always turns out badly for us, because now the red monsignor has come and excommunicated us. And since in truth we aren't certain whether hell exists or not, that remains so until we are pushing up rubber plants, we don't really know if these bastards are sending us to hell or not. The truth is we don't know. But the American tells us that the true religion is the religion of Christ, theirs; and that the priests messed it up ever since a Communist pope came on the scene, whom they certainly poisoned through the influence they have; and even with a pope who is anticommunist they say that's still very bad, but even so we can't be certain, since the Catholics have already allied themselves with Armageddon. You don't believe me, friend, perhaps because they're keeping you in the dark: the Communists and the priests have already won you over. That's why we have to sacrifice ourselves by having to kill so many sons of bitches. The poorer they are the more they're sons of bitches. And you know that very well, buddy. Before, everything was quite alright, nobody was going around stirring up things and they didn't go around talking about things like minimum wage; why don't they ask once and for all for the maximum wage and put an end to all that bull. Imagine, they are now wanting to have cheese to eat. But Armageddon will soon come to do away with this whole race, that is if it's not among us already saving us. When in their whoring and Catholic lives had they eaten cheese? We even get belly-aches when we eat anything but tortillas, salt, and beans. But we have so many sons of bitches in this country coming to enlist us to demand from the rich something that's not within their power to give us. Look, buddy, don't upset me, you shouldn't want to get mad at me for eating the things I told you about; I have to eat well. That's why I didn't want to tell you anything. What I do is in the line of duty; and, besides, I belong to the armies of God, because we're saving civilization, not with any damned ideas that come in books but with daily practice, using the resources of the most civilized country on earth. We go about praying to God and using the big stick. Look, if you want to we'll have another drink, but now I'll pay, so they won't say that I've turned out bad. I know that you civilians believe that we are brutes and we only know how to handle guns, but as you see, we also have our ideas. In that way we are sure that nobody's going to brainwash us.

Hey, don't quit on me, I've had twice as much as you and I'm still sober, but you've already become a fruit, don't be offended. And don't be angry at me because then you'll just have the trouble of calming yourself down. Just a beer, my friend, to hold down the liquor.

You see what you're doing, while I pour myself double shots, you play the maiden aunt and only sip a little bit. You want me to lose control so you can say afterwards that I couldn't hold my liquor, so you can go around putting me down. Anyway, my friend, I promise I won't insult you anymore, so drink up the beer.

You know, with regard to brainwashing, I told the American: look, I thought that brainwashing was done with hog soap and water. And everybody burst out laughing. Except the American, who is a superserious person. He doesn't joke with anybody.

And he told me: You're right, it's like washing it with soap, any kind of soap, it doesn't matter. What you understood about brainwashing is good enough, he told us: because it is a very complicated scientific problem. It isn't simple, my friend. That's how it is, with us being an underdeveloped country, we are a bunch of ignoramuses. We stopped asking questions but my friends kept on laughing. Then the American said: "Shut up, you sons of bitches." And you should see how well he uses that expression, it's one of the first ones he learned, he told us one day, and I think we are going to use it very often. At that time we didn't understand what he meant by using it very often. Afterwards we came to understand clearly, since all he calls us is sons of bitches and worse. One day he explained to us that it was a part of the norms of discipline, that we should get used to it, and that we also would know how to use it when it became necessary, and in a natural way.

Look, once the American flies off the handle no one can stop him, he lets loose a storm, a storm of shit, nothing ordinary, because from the beginning the director told us that the American had complete authority just as the Chinaman eats "lice," and is free to give us a kick in the ass when we don't understand the things he says. So that you can see I am sincere, I'll tell you that just as there are great pleasures, there are also those things that at first we don't get accustomed to easily.

One doesn't fool around with the American, my friend. Nor with the Chinaman. They're here to make us men and to understand the problems of Communism in this backward country. I would like to see you getting a kick in the ass or a karate chop in the nape of the neck from the little Chinaman. Because if your eyes begin to close in class, if you begin to doze off, forget it; the Chinaman comes up on you from behind and pow! the chop in your neck. Let me tell you that more than one of my classmates have gone directly to the hospital and not come back. That's how it is, my friend, and what else can you do? It's worse to be eating shit here, knocking yourself out from sunrise to sunset for wages that don't even provide for sufficient food. The reality is that you were born to become a beast, my friend. They haven't even taught you right or you wouldn't be telling me those things. And if I excuse you it's because of your ignorance. But don't doubt that I can send you away from here in a bag; it's for that kind of thing that I'm being trained in the Special Forces.

I wouldn't have mercy on my mother or my father, let alone a friend.

The truth is that all civilians are shit, my friend, and you are no exception. You all envy our uniform, the fact that we have moved up in life.

That's why when we have to act we don't spare anyone. Did you hear me my friend?

from PULSE
Ricardo Humano

And doesn't it happen to you
that after
so much talking
you become dizzy?

from SOME SAYINGS AND DEEDS
Nachín

Other characters join the fray.
Pompous asses trained to negotiate with their own
        consciences.
Those who couldn't wait to be ministers.
The self-worshippers who base their lives on farce.
The chubby ones whose bodies discharge deathly odour.
The poisonous sly ones.
Those who walk after bones.
Those who needed only a gentle push
to fall on their knees,
"at your unconditional orders, my colonel."
The poor wretches who say
"we pay only so much for 100 kilos,"
when they speak protectively of the accounts of
        the oligarchs.
The belly-full-heart-contented ones.

from EPITAPH
Rolando Costa

I also see how they go away satiated
belching and grumbling
hiding from each other the private road
to the profound bed
or to the lavatory
the shade of the biggest tree
or the deepest ravine

I also see how the flies follow them

THE POLICE AND THE GUARDS
Roque Dalton

They always saw the people
as a mass of shoulders running here and there
as a field on which to let truncheons of hatred have
          free play.

They always saw the people through the eye they used
          to sharpen their aim
and between the people and the eye
the pistol or rifle-sight.

(Once they too were people
but with the excuse of hunger and unemployment
they accepted a gun
a truncheon and a monthly salary
to defend the starvers and the unemployers.)

They always saw the people enduring
sweating
shouting
raising signs
raising their fists
and at the most telling them:
"Your turn will come you mean sons of bitches."

(And with each passing day
they thought they had pulled off a big deal
by betraying the people of whom they were born:
"The people are a pile of silly weaklings" — they thought —
"how well we did by crossing over to the side of the
          vigorous and the strong.")

And then it was time to squeeze the trigger
and the bullets went from the side of the police and the
      Civil Guard
over to the side of the people
that is the way
they always went
from over there to over here
and the people fell bleeding to death
week after week year after year
shattered bones
the people wept through the eyes of women and children
and fleeing frightened
stopped being people to become a scarlet-coloured
      shambles
the survivors disappeared however they could each one
      heading for home
and then nothing more
except that firemen washed the blood from the streets.

(The colonels had convinced them:
"That's it boys" — they told them —
"hit hard at the heads of the civilians
treat the mob to fire
you are also uniformed pillars of the Nation
priests of the first rank
of the cult of the flag the coat of arms the anthem of
      great leaders
representative democracy the official party and the
      free world

the decent people of this country will not forget
        your sacrifices
even though right now we can't raise your salaries
as we really want to do.")

They always saw the people twitching in the torture room
hanging
beaten
fractured
swollen
suffocated
raped
pricked by needles in their ears and eyes
electrified
drowned in urine and excrement
spat on
dragged about
their last remains giving off little smoke bubbles
in the hell of quick lime.

(When the tenth National Guard was put out of action
        by the people
and the fifth police precinct was unravelled by the
        urban guerrillas
the policemen and the National Guardsmen began
        to think
primarily about how the colonels had changed their tune
and that today for every failure they blamed
"our terribly unreliable fighting forces.")

The fact is that the police and the Guards
always saw the people over here from over there
and the bullets always came from over there to over here.
Let them think hard about it
let them decide themselves whether it is too late
to seek the side of the people
and shoot from over here
shoulder to shoulder beside us.

Let them think hard about it
but in the meantime
let them not seem surprised
or worse look offended
now that some bullets
are already beginning to get to them from this side
where the people remain the same as always
except that at this stage what they do is heart-felt
and they carry more and more guns.

from *THE INFINITE HEADS*
Roberto Monterroza

Memorable visions are approaching
not for the fat ones surfeited on meat
and their fine homes,
simply for the saddest-eyed girl.

MAMMA TINA'S HANDS
Gabriela Yanes

Mamma Tina's hands are those of a dressmaker who is dedicated to love. Other equally soft hands sketch in the air a cloud that smiles at seeing itself created in the midst of tropical verdure.

Mamma Tina occupies a small hidden space in San Salvador (from her kitchen she hears gunshots going off in Zacamil, from her window she sees the parade of the dead early every morning). She is growing old in these changing times.

Meanwhile, in the hills her granddaughter intones a rumba-like song, out of love she disperses a cloud, she gives shape to a smile and shoots with the hands she inherited from Mamma Tina.

from *HALLELUJAH FLOATING HEAD
LIKE A TRAPEZOIDAL MOON*
Roberto Monterroza

Hallelujah floating head like a trapezoidal moon
the green horses chew the tobacco's insanity
gold pins in the lapel in the corner of suspicion
walls in the city
beautiful gypsy girl piece of my heart
drunk with chicha
it was a lovely morning dawning with bright stars
hallelujah floating head
God help us in the violent wind

from *ORGANIZED POETRY*
Róger Lindo

Tinplate blue the sky
intrepid discovery
that drags the day along

We clean poetry
with relative surrender
revitalized
by the good operation of the morning

poorly supported by six
tiny and pitiful missiles

Blue without lunar butter
little olive-green bells
sewing bristles in the countryside
approach igniting the tender air

Poetry, colour of the surroundings
combat presses it more and more
against the wind

from CRUMBS
Claudia Lars

I was slow to hear the rebels' footsteps
and the live burial of any prison.
Today I am ashamed of the years wasted
in the comfortable refuge
of the deaf.

from *LATER POEMS*
Eduardo Sancho Casteñada

keep the master vessel
the best part of man is in the potter's wheel
when it casts moulds

GET UP JUANA SPIRITS
Alfonso Quijada Urías

Get up Juana Spirits,
Get up Miguel, Miguel Skirmish.
The Yankees are here.
Get out your scorpions Juana Spirits,
your urine that blinds.
Drive them crazy with your powders
and make the streets swallow them.
Get up Miguel, Miguel Skirmish.
Before the cock crows
and the owl flies,
drive your thorns into them,
your poisoned goods.
Shake your calabashes Juana Spirits,
invoke the fierceness of your angered gods.
May the air suffocate them,
may the sun reduce them to ashes,
may a sunbeam turn them into road stones.
Get up Miguel,
Miguel Skirmish
with your tough boys,
makers of traps,
hunters with slingshots, relatives of the jaguar;
hurl your serpents, your aggressive stones at them
before their airplanes can continue spewing napalm.
Wake up Juana Spirits,
Wake up Miguel,
the new day approaches
cleaner than yesterday
and there is a lot of fire,
a whole lot of fire to stoke.

ADVISER
Horacio Castellanos Moya

Roy Prosterman, North American, brilliant
professional, arrived in San Salvador.

Roy Prosterman, some years ago, in Saigon,
became the lover of an ex-director of the CIA
named Colby: together they conceived
"Operation Phoenix"
to murder thousands of Vietnamese;
but even with their "strategic hamlets"
they fled Vietnam completely routed.

Roy Prosterman, oracle of the Junta,
minister of the "agrarian reform,"
needs North American and Saigonese advisers
because to him Latin American military men
have always seemed to be too stupid.

Roy Prosterman, in the very near future,
just as in Vietnam,
will board his plane hurriedly,
with some other thousands of corpses in his suitcase
he will show up in Washington.

That is if we don't seize him...

THE DAY
Miguel Huezo Mixco

The sun has already arrived
armed
like a combatant.

Enthused I jump
from sleep
naked
like a sword.

from CONCERNING LOVE
Lil Milagro Ramírez

I saw you leave yesterday with bullets and paint
You kissed me on returning

from SONG TO LIBERTY AND HAPPINESS
Luiz Díaz

You have said new things this time
silence has been broken
by sweet rosy words.

We must expect more
and better songs.

from FOR A BETTER LOVE
Roque Dalton

Everybody agrees that sex
is a category in the world of lovers:
thus its tenderness and savage branches.

Everybody agrees that sex
is an economic category:
you have only to mention prostitution,
fashion,
the newspaper sections that are only for her
or only for him.

The trouble begins
when a woman says
that sex is a political category.

Because when a woman says
that sex is a political category
she can begin to stop being a woman as such
and become a woman for herself,
to make the woman into a woman
on the basis of her humanity
and not of her sex,
to know that the magical lemon-flavoured deodorant
and the soap that voluptuously caresses her skin
are made by the same firm that makes napalm,
to know that the basic household tasks
are the basic tasks of the social class of the household,
that the difference of sexes
shines much better in the profound amorous night
when all those secrets are known
that had us wearing masks and estranged.

WELL, YES, OF COURSE!
Mauricio Marquina

The simple and intense fraternity
is the vibrant poetry of this daily
struggle.

from a novel in preparation
Manuel Sorto

The old woman had half-closed her eyes. Sebastián
thought that would make a good picture, with the old
woman exhibiting her elephantitis and with her black
coat soiled by the swallows against the neoromantic fa-
çade of the recently remodelled theatre and with that
background of walls full of graffiti in black, red, and yellow: FAPU — FTC — JOIN THE PEOPLE'S MILITIA — LP-28 —
GOVERNMENT SHIT — BPR — PCS — ARMED STRUGGLE TO-
DAY SOCIALISM TOMORROW all in a festival of acronyms
and numbers. The old men were asleep reclining against
the graffiti to the left of the old woman. The only thing
needed now was to get the manager of the theatre to
pose, in this scene of San Salvador daily life, in his casual
British clothes. Sebastián took advantage of the light being
red to cross the street and go over to Morazán square.

The sun had started to beat down hard. The burning pavement was baking his feet through the worn soles of his moccasins. Some banners and placards from the most recent demonstration still hung from Morazán's statue. Sebastián's eyes moved from the red banner of the BPR that adorned the left arm and half of Morazán's chest to the windows on the second floor of the Alcázar Bar. The only time he had seen Manso Eduardo drink had been there. What would Manso be doing now? He felt like going to have a nice cold beer by one of the windows of the old wooden building. No, he told himself. Today you are not going to drink. He went into the crowd. At the corner of Primera Poniente Street he took a look at the front page of the newspaper *El Independiente:* DUARTE DECLARES THAT HE IS NOT AFRAID OF THE PEOPLE. What a fine headline, he thought, they really messed him up. He bought it.

He felt his body being kneaded along with the many others that were making their way as well as they could along the narrow sidewalk. Two blind men were going wild with a guitar and a hornpipe. A dog sitting on its hindlegs was listening to them very intently. He thought that the dog could have been trained to function as an audience and attract the sheep. The dog turned its head and observed him closely, as if it had divined his thinking. The people continued hurriedly without stopping to look at the musicians. A fat lady, in her haste, pushed him. The fruit vendors exchanged shouts at the edge of the gutter, while they fanned themselves with paper bags. The beggars were leaning against the wall, protecting themselves from the sun and the motor cars. Some drunkards and unemployed, made motionless by the heat, controlled the roads. He distinguished among the strong mixture of smells that of a recently bathed little child. The Cathedral loudspeaker (captured for how long?) could be heard clearly: **The people, united, will never be defeated.**

The people...and the smells smearing his skin and the women walking rhythmically with their baskets balanced on their heads, and the vendors of combs and magazines and nail clippers and children's undershirts, all pushing their merchandise into his face. An anxious little boy, barefooted and shirtless, took him by the hand and didn't let him go until he had given him money. He began to sweat. He felt someone touch him below the waist and saw a young boy in an orange-coloured Nehru shirt, plucked eyebrows and Mia Farrow type hair tinged with yellow, throwing him a kiss. A truck with guards had stopped opposite the Lutecia Bar. One of the guards was observing him carefully, but what made him nervous was the eye of the G-3.

The light turned green and the truck moved on. "The beast frightened you, eh!" someone behind him shouted. He turned around. Opposite the New World Hotel on the other side of the street, Pocho was looking at him, smiling. He was holding in his hand a snack of sliced green mango which the vendor had just sprinkled with pumpkin-seed powder and crushed red peppers. A bandaid covered his left eye, his right ear was purple and inflamed. "So the beast frightened you!" Pocho shouted again. Both of them burst out laughing. The vendor joined in.

They were walking along First Street toward San José Park. Pocho was asking so many questions that Sebastián felt dazed. What are you doing? Where are you living? Can you get good marijuana? Sebastián replied with monosyllables and evasions. On reaching General Electric Street Pocho stopped. He seemed to have remembered the sliced mango and he offered it to Sebastián. He kept looking at the building for which the street was named.

"Do you like it?" he asked.

"Well, I don't know."

"These buildings were constructed between the end of the last century and the beginning of this one. They used sheets of steel in their construction because of the earthquakes."

Sebastián observed Pocho somewhat curiously. He took a look at the building, faking an interest that he did not manage to sustain because of a girl who was passing in tight jeans. "Pretty," said Pocho, without losing his interest in the building. "And just imagine," he continued, "it was a Turk who started this business, because I don't know if you know that the incredible thing about this craziness is that all the parts were brought by boat from Europe." Pocho shared the last strips of mango and threw away the paper.

"They are like the buildings on Arce Street, the Basilica, for example," Pocho continued. Sebastián was cleaning the remains of red pepper and pumpkin-seed powder from his fingers, not knowing whether to laugh or not at the seriousness in Pocho's lecture.

"They have their charm, these buildings," Pocho added with the tone of an oracle, "some of them tend to the late Gothic."

Sebastián couldn't suppress his laughter, which was immediately silenced by the engine of another truck carrying guards.

"Don't panic," said Pocho, "it is better not to pay any attention to these sons of bitches. If they realize you're scared they begin to give you hell." From Cathedral Square could be heard:...**disappear, disappear**.... They crossed the street. Something strange was going on. The people who were at the corner of San José Park began to run. Many others ran toward them. Suddenly a burst of machine-gun fire was heard.

"The nastiness has begun!"

Another burst rang out. Then some isolated shots. The shopkeepers hurriedly pulled down the metal doors of their businesses. Some of those who were fleeing managed to enter before the doors closed. The bursts of machine-gun fire continued. Other isolated shots were heard replying dryly, one after the other. The traffic noise which a moment earlier was monotonous had become filled with roars, and shrieks of tires. Sebastián noticed above all else the sound of the feet of the crowd moving rapidly over the pavement. Pocho nudged him on the shoulder and they ran back to the corner of General Electric Street.

"What's going on today?" shouted Sebastián.

"The secondary students are trying to leave the ministry!" The street was pure panic.

"To Hardees!" Pocho shouted on reaching the corner.

A group of student demonstrators passed by the Central Café. One of them carried a little pistol that looked like a toy. Two women beat with their fists on the door of Caruso's, which was almost closed. Don't close! Don't close! With a loud crash the door closed completely. The vendors ran with their baskets, their children, and their stools, stumbling into people. Shoes, ear-rings, handkerchiefs, and fruits went flying and were strewn about the street. The bursts of machine-gun fire wouldn't cease and were sounding ever closer. A child propelled by the crowd bounced off the wall and crashed against the sidewalk. "Damn it," Pocho moaned and dashed toward the child, but one of the armed young men darted from among the people and seized the boy by one arm, hoisting him to his shoulders without slowing down. "Long live self-defence!" shouted a young man. Pocho rejoined Sebastián, who waited for him, stunned and not knowing what to do. Together they headed toward Hardees and almost collided with an old woman who was slowly picking up her basket of sweets and cigarettes.

"Treacherous sons of bitches!" the old woman cried. "The boys had already arranged things with the minister and that's why they were leaving! But the dogs were waiting for them!"

The bullets were whizzing by too close.

"Don't play the fool Grandma, get down!" shouted Pocho, and shielding her with his body he dragged her behind a car. Sebastián watched them as he took cover behind a door. The shooting stopped. The people took advantage of that to seek better protection. Pocho forced the old woman to take better cover, looked about him and ran over to Sebastián.

"Hardees is closed..."

"Yes, damn it, I know."

Again the machine-guns rang out and the bullets bounced along the pavement. A little girl, head down, crossed the street. She slipped and fell at the edge of the gutter, with her hand bleeding. A boy ran to the sidewalk on the other side of the street, took cover behind a car and began to shoot in the direction of the flat roofs. Sebastián could make out the snipers hiding on the roofs, in their light blue shirts like those worn by bank employees. Another boy ran to the centre of the street and also shot at the roofs. As he shot he did a kind of dance to shield the wounded girl. Two other boys approached the girl and dragged her behind a car. The dancer, continuing to shoot and dance, went back to the door. The old woman whom Pocho had protected managed to go over to where the girl was being treated. She carefully took her head and placed it on her lap. The shooting stopped once more. Sebastián was looking transfixed at the little girl. One of those treating her turned toward his comrades and shook his head sadly. The old woman rested the little girl's head on her breast. A tear trickled from Sebastián's eye. "Let us try to reach Bella Nápoles," Pocho whispered. They ran crouching. New bursts of gunfire obliged them to take refuge behind some cars where a few comrades of the self-defence group were taking cover. The girl sobbed, her little body tightly contracted. One of the comrades caressed her head. "Don't cry, don't cry," he told her, "your mother is somewhere nearby, don't worry, everything will soon be alright." The little girl seemed to gasp for air between her tears. Now the bullets were hurling themselves into the car that was shielding them. The comrades returned the fire. Sebastián caressed the head of the little girl. On the roof one of the sky-blue shirts turned into a red explosion.

"Do you have guns, comrades?" asked one of the boys.

"Damn it," mumbled Pocho.

"Then you have to move from here. Don't compromise us."

The comrades of the self-defence group looked at each other for awhile. They seemed to come to a decision.

"Try to leave this street, we will cover you. Take the little girl with you."

"Run when we tell you," said the other one.

The comrade observed the roofs for a few seconds. He took a look at the street corners. He whistled loudly. From further ahead came another whistle in reply. The comrade jumped toward the centre of the street, shooting. Some twenty metres away another comrade did the same thing and zigzagged in the middle of the street. Sebastián felt someone tug at his shirt and he ran off carrying the little child in his arms. Pocho followed him. A puff of gunfire swept the pavement and a cold chill passed over Sebastián's back. Pocho pushed him into a doorway. Sebastián fell face down trying to protect the girl's head as well as he could.

"Shit, it's closed!"

They could see through the glass how, inside the cafe, people were huddled together behind tables that had been placed in front of the shop window. A waitress tried to make the metal curtain work. The child moaned and tightened her hold on Sebastián's neck. Pocho knocked on the shop window. The comrades of the self-defence group took cover again behind the cars. Except for a few pauses the firing seemed interminable. An old woman prayed, stooping behind a door. Finally there was silence. They ran toward La Dalia. A stampede of people hurled them back against the Bella Nápoles shop window. They heard explosions. At the corner of Oriani some cars burst into flames. The little girl had stopped crying. A puff of gunfire hit a woman next to them. Her shattered head crashed against the wall. "Don't move!" whispered Pocho. A new blast smashed into the wall above their heads. Again, silence. A moan there. A sob. The child's little body tightened against Sebastián's chest. The door of Bella Nápoles opened. "Hurry!" urged Pocho, pushing Sebastián who struggled along with the girl as best he could. A new blast. A woman who was about to take the girl screamed, looking outside. Sebastián turned around. Pocho's body streaming blood flew through the air. A hard thump resounded against the wall. Another one on the sidewalk. A part of his body was seen spinning toward the gutter. Pocho's face was a bloody void. The door was closed. The phosphorescence of the wall clock said it was twenty to one.

from FEVER
Miguel Huezo Mixco

I can imagine the city
stuck to the ground like a playing card
about to explode with fury
at this precise moment
I hate this city
No soldier loves his trench
He loves instead the other world
He loves the idea of something new
replacing what is travelling readily to its quick death
under the pain of a sun ray
shredded by lightning bolts
beheaded
fearless of falling to pieces.

from THE WAR CHEWS UP THE DAYS
Horacio Castellanos Moya

The war chews up the days
much to the displeasure of our longings,
it pushes us to dubious defences,
to somewhat hackneyed verses.
An intelligent optimism is demanded of us but,
    sometimes,
the simple sound of a guitar,
the mere night entering monotonously,
the malaise due to too much coffee as we converse,
    in brief,
any minimal circumstance
becomes the precise justification for my sitting down
in front of my typewriter.

from an interview
Carlos Antonio Gómez
_____

...I am a watch repairman by profession.

At the camp they taught me to handle guns, to operate in urban zones and we set off explosions in several towns. After a month, they gave me a course in anti-guerrilla operations. Many of my friends went to Panama for training. I didn't. I also received paramilitary training and learned many tactics of attack and withdrawal. They gave us camouflaged uniforms and North American-made boots.

Precisely on Soldier's Day we welcomed the Green Berets who came from the United States. The high command told us that the new arrivals would teach us new tactics. Prior to this we had paid homage to the fallen soldiers.

We were given classes on the Vietnam war and on how we should act on the battlefield. They told us that we shouldn't feel compassion for anyone; even if they were children or old people. We should kill everyone.

The courses on torture began. One afternoon they brought in nine youths accused of being guerrillas. The first one, who was between fifteen and sixteen years old, said all kinds of things that should have led them to set him free. The Green Berets didn't speak Spanish, but a Salvadorean officer translated for us. They began to torture the boy by sticking knives into his nails. Then they pulled out his nails and broke one of his elbows. Right after that, a Green Beret plucked out his eyes and made all sorts of incisions in the skin of his chest, his arms, and his legs. After that they held him by his hair and scalped him. When they saw that there was nothing left to do with him they poured gasoline over him and burned him. The next day his corpse was found in the street.

Then they began to do almost the same thing to a thirteen-year-old girl. They undressed her and threw her into a little room: one by one all the officers raped her. Later they brought her out tied and with her eyes blindfolded. Then they started the mutilation: they pulled out her nails and cut off her fingers. They also broke her arms and gouged out her eyes, like they did to the boy. Lastly, they cut off her legs and applied a red-hot iron to her belly...

The last boy they killed that day suffered much more. They undressed him and put him on a hot metal sheet. It was as if they were frying him alive. After half an hour, when they finally took him off, he was covered with wounds. Then they threw him into the sea, bound, still alive, from a helicopter.

Some days later the Green Berets took us to a volcano that is a guerrilla stronghold. The Green Berets didn't fight but stayed behind telling us how to do it. They criticized our errors. We spent five days up at the volcano. Many of the soldiers didn't come back; they died.

About twenty-five days after the Green Berets arrived, while I was on guard, hundreds of munitions disappeared. They imprisoned me and, later, tortured me. Although they didn't cut me up like they did the guerrillas, they broke my wrist and my left leg with blows. They locked me up in a cell where there were several guerrillas.

After many conversations with the young people in the cell I asked them what I should do. Then I found out that one of the officers was working in co-ordination with the guerrilla movement.

Some days later the officer came to the cell and told me: "Trust me and you will leave here." I asked him what I should do. "You have a brother who is a guerrilla." He called my brother's name. He told me I should escape, that if I died it would be while fighting, but against imperialism, not against the people. "How?" I asked again. "You will see this afternoon," he told me, "you won't be the only one."

We began the escape at seven-thirty p.m. We were getting ready to leave when a guard fired a shot and raised the alarm. The confrontation started. We had a lot of ammunition, submachine-guns and M-16 rifles. Nearing midnight we were still unable to escape. But we finally mastered the situation, and we set off toward Chalatenango. The guerrilla army was waiting for us, since they knew we were going to desert that night. From our group a corporal and one soldier died, another corporal was severely wounded. I was also wounded.

Litanies of the Holy Women
Rafael Mendoza

Don't hurt him, cold, with your scales!
Night, stick no dagger into him!
Saints of the roadways, take care of my son!
Protect him always from evil!

Seven goats feeding in the hills,
light up his dream, for pity's sake!
Night owl that never sleeps,
tell him of the dangers he may encounter!

Saints of the roadways, take care of my son!
Protect him always from evil!

Oh, miraculous ruda plant, give him luck!
Touch him for me if he passes, with your power!
Climbing plants, cover with your vines
my poor boy! Cover him well!

Saints of the roadways, take care of my son!
Protect him always from evil!

Oh quails, fly when the murderer guards
appear with their G-threes!
lizard of the hills, jump noisily
if the patrol comes near him!

Saints of the roadways, take care of my son!
Protect him always from evil!

Oh, San Bartolomé de Perulapía
tell your Black Christ to bring him back to me!
If you do me that favour I will light
you a candle in my hut and another on your altar!

Saints of the roadways, take care of my son!
Protect him always from evil!

Oh, if they kill my son because of his convictions,
grant me at least that they hand him over to me
so I can bury him beside his father.

Saints of the roadways, take care of my son!
Protect him always from evil!
Don't expose him to danger!
Listen to these his mother's pleas!

from the song THE PEOPLE WASH THEIR FACES
Paco Barrios

Some soldiers passed by
they passed by over there
but in your bosom
I was hidden.

SERENADE FOR REFUGEE CHILDREN
Rafael Mendoza

Tell me, most excellent bright star,
do you light up my country from there?...

The eyes of the dead are lighting it up.
I see them from here...

Tell me, old friend Mr. Summer,
are there kites now in the wind over there?...

There are kites and vultures on the watch;
and there are more vultures...

Tell me Mr. Winter, sad sir,
how many of our rebels are you wetting?...

I cannot count them for they are many;
and I quench their thirst...

Tell me, little dove that goes and comes,
when will you bring good news?...

Oh my! It is difficult for a people to win their freedom...
Yours will win!

from the song LOS TOROGOCES
Los Torogoces de Morazán

Over there in the hills
a voice is heard
it is the happy song
of the torogoz bird

Very early in the morning
it begins its song
wake up brother
our work day has begun

The man from Barranquilla
works with great ardour
Just like the guerrilla
from El Salvador

Testimony of Comandante Sebastían
Carlos Aragón

On Tuesday January 26 they informed me that we would be going into action that night. When we were all concentrated at a point quite close to the target, we still didn't know whether it was going to be a preliminary exercise or whether we were really going to carry out the plan. It was seven p.m. when Alejandro came with the go-ahead, and I explained to the comrades that, in fact, it would be that night.

We began to go over the final details of the mission with each comrade. Even with all the previous reconnoitering and all our preparations it was necessary to do that, because on hardly any two nights were the planes and helicopters placed in the same way on the airstrip. They kept changing their disposition in order to avoid any risks. At that time we already had the exact plan of the placement of the airplanes that night, and on the basis of this plan we decided on the details.

At ten we began the approach to the base. You should know that on the south side of the air force base there is steep cliff, which is like a natural barrier and very difficult to climb.

At exactly twelve the nine of us who formed the advance command reached the boundary of the base. We had three teams for assistance and security, which had earlier taken up positions in different places. They were three teams of five combatants each, with vehicles and fire-power, but we had no communication with them. For the operation we could count on no outside help; their only function was to guarantee our withdrawal.

When we reached the boundary we checked again to

see if everything corresponded with what we knew before, whether they had changed anything in their security system.

At that stage there was no possibility of our discussing anything, the slightest word or any other type of communication was prohibited.

We were ten metres from one of the guard posts, we could hear the soldiers talking. The whole area was lit up, both inside and outside, but we had great confidence in our technique and in the fact that the other side never thought of the possibility of a silent penetration, but only of an attack launched from outside.

The whole plan was to penetrate, place the charges, and leave without being detected. We carried UZI weapons, but with orders not to use them under any circumstances, unless we were detected, were all surrounded, and there was no other possibility of withdrawing.

We had divided the command into three teams of two each, which had to reach the machines and place the charges. The rest served as security: Vitilio and Vigil at an advanced point and Heriberto ten metres from the guard post. Samuel, the political representative of the command, and Henry went first. They went along the inside area; when they didn't return within two minutes, Rigo and I advanced; César and Emerson went immediately after.

Each team had its defined route. The time was determined by a mechanism in the charges we carried. It was calculated so as to enable us to advance the three hundred metres from the guard post to the airplanes; we had ten minutes to place the charges and an adequate time for the withdrawal, which we had to make in the same silent manner.

As we passed by another garrison, we heard one of the guards checking his gun. We waited a while without moving, but nothing happened.

The patrol jeep passed every five minutes, sometimes at a distance of only a few metres.

We had no contact with the others; we only knew where they were supposed to be advancing.

We saw the helicopters first. They were very close to the barracks, not more than fifty metres away, and we could hear the soldiers' chatter. There were two companies there, one of them made up of paratroopers.

Twenty-five metres away were the Ouragans, placed tightly together in a row and, with more space between them, the C-47s and the Fouga Magisters.

There were more airplanes in the eastern sector, but we were not to touch those. The concentration was close to the barracks and it was on those planes that we placed the charges, five and a half kilos of TNT.

We kept precisely to the ten minutes we had for placing the charges on the planes. Then we left in the same order in which we had entered. We did all this in a synchronized manner and each team left by the indicated exit.

Just as we crossed the boundary of the base, we heard the first explosion. It was three minutes past one.

Two minutes later a helicopter approached; it had taken off from the same base, where they always have an airplane and a helicopter at combat readiness, parked well to the east of the zone where we had operated.

They started to fire immediately from the helicopter, but wildly, without any target. For about an hour they flew over the zone and tried to locate us by firing tracer bullets.

We could still see the helicopter when we reached the place where one of the teams of assistance was waiting for us with vehicles.

We left the zone before the arrival of the thousands of troops who were sent that same night to search the whole region adjoining the base.

It was in this way that we cut the junta's wings.

BECAUSE I WANT PEACE
Claribel Alegría

Because I want peace
and not war
because I don't want to see
hungry children
or emaciated women
or men with silenced
tongues
I must keep on fighting.

Because there are
clandestine
cemeteries
Death Squads
and White Hand
that torture
that maim
that murder
I want to keep on fighting.
Because on the mountain range
of Guazapa
from their hideouts
my brothers lie in wait for
three battalions
trained in Carolina
and Georgia
I must keep on fighting.
Because from armed Huey
helicopters
expert pilots
wipe out villages
with napalm
poison the water
and burn the crops
that feed the people
I want to keep on fighting.
Because there are territories
now liberated
where those who don't know how to
are learning to read
and the sick are treated
and the produce of the land
belongs to everybody
I must keep on fighting.
Because I want peace
and not war.

from THE WAR WE ARE GOING TO WIN
Manuel Sorto

Our war deserves
the tenderest caresses
the sweetest songs
the cleanest words

NOTES FOR THE INTRODUCTION

1 The notes and authorial identification in this English-language edition are a necessary encroachment on this pattern. The collection was originally put together in Spanish as *Fragmentos de la actual literatura salvadoreña*, Querétaro, Mexico: Universidad Nacional de Querétaro, 1983. For this edition one poem, the penultimate one, has been added by the translator.

2 James Dunkerley, *The Long War: Dictatorship and Revolution in El Salvador*, London: Junction Books, 1982; pp. 10-11. Some other excellent general studies of the causes and conduct of the hostilities in El Salvador are: Liisa North, *Bitter Grounds: Roots of Revolt in El Salvador*, Toronto: Between The Lines, 1981, 2nd edition, 1985; Robert Armstrong and Janet Shenk, *El Salvador: Face of Revolution*, Boston: South End Press, 1982; Cynthia Arnson, *El Salvador: A Revolution Confronts the United States*, Washington, D.C.: Institute for Policy Studies, 1982; Tommie Sue Montgomery, *Revolution in El Salvador: Origins and Evolution*, Boulder, Colorado: Westview Press, 1982; Walter LaFeber, *Inevitable Revolutions: The United States in Central America*, New York: Norton, 1983; Raymond Bonner, *Weakness and Deceit: The United States Policy and El Salvador*, New York: Times Books, 1984; Charles Clements, *Free Fire Zone: An American Doctor in El Salvador*, New York: Bantam Books, 1984.

3 For a collection of essays that deal with the theoretical and historical bases of these developments, see Roberto Fernández Retamar, *Para el perfil definitivo del hombre*, La Habana: Editorial Letras Cubanas, 1981.

4 R.D.F. Pring-Mill, "The Scope of Spanish American Committed Poetry," *Homenaje a Rodolfo Grossmann*, ed. Sabine Horl et al., Frankfurt: Verlag Peter Lang, 1977, pp. 259-333.

5 See, for example, *Poesía campesina de Solentiname*, selection and prologue by Mayra Jiménez, Managua: Ministerio de Cultura, 1980; and *Poesía de la nueva Nicaragua*, selection and prologue by Mayra Jiménez, introduction by Ernesto Cardenal, Mexico: Siglo Veintiuno Editores, 1983.

6 *Antología general de la poesía en El Salvador*, selection, prologue and notes by José Roberto Cea, San Salvador: Editorial Universitaria de El Salvador, 1971, p. 7.

7 *Homenaje a El Salvador,* introduction by Claribel Alegría, prologue by Julio Cortázar, Madrid: Visor, 1981.

8 Roque Dalton's work has only recently become available in translation in North America. See Roque Dalton, *Poemas clandestinos/Clandestine poems,* introduction by Margaret Randall, San Francisco: Solidarity Publications, 1984; and *Roque Dalton,* trans. Richard Schaaf, Willimantic, Conn.: Curbstone Press, 1984.

9 *Poesía contemporánea de Centro América,* selection and notes by Roberto Armijo and Rigoberto Paredes, Barcelona: Los libros de la Frontera, 1983.

10 Ibid., p. 19.

11 *Poesía de El Salvador,* selection, notes and prologue by Manlio Argueta, San José: EDUCA, 1983.

12 Manlio Argueta, *One Day of Life,* trans. Bill Brow, New York: Vintage, 1983.

Notes on the Text

p. 17, line 2: Gachupin is a nickname given Spaniards who established themselves in Spanish America.

p. 17, line 5: Malinche was the Indian interpreter for and lover of the Spanish conquistador Hernán Cortés.

p. 17, line 13: Panchimalco is an Indian city near San Salvador.

p. 17, line 17: The "pito" is a plant that bears a fruit resembling the penis. Its leaves produce a soporific drink when boiled.

p. 18, line 6: Pedro de Alvarado was a Spanish conquistador, a former lieutenant of Cortés, who waged devastating wars against the Indians of Central America.

p. 25, line 2: Anastasio Aquino was a worker on an indigo estate who led a revolt of peasants in 1833. See Introduction.

p. 41, line 1: This poem refers to General Maximiliano Hernández Martínez, in power during the 1932 *matanza*, or "slaughter," which saw the deaths of an estimated 30,000 peasants.

p. 58, line 10: One colón equals forty cents.

p. 67, line 1: The "humble little priest" refers to Archbishop Oscar Romero. See Introduction.

p. 83, line 3: Two of Jaime Suárez Quemain's poems are included in this collection. See also Biographical Notes.

p. 116, line 7: FAPU: United Popular Action Front.
FTC: Federation of Rural Workers.
LP-28: Popular Leagues — 28 February.

p. 116, line 8: BPR: Popular Revolutionary Bloc.
PCS: Communist Party of El Salvador.

p. 116, line 15: Francisco Morazán, a Honduran, was the second and last president of the United Provinces of Central America. The union ended in 1839 and Morazán was forced to leave San Salvador in 1840. The Republic of El Salvador got its name in 1841.

p. 130, line 3: The ruda is a Salvadorean plant said to possess magical properties.

p. 133, line 9: Barranquilla is a city in Colombia.

Biographical Notes

Claribel Alegría (b. 1924) was born in Nicaragua but grew up in El Salvador. She has travelled widely in Europe, North America, and Latin America. Now living in Managua, she considers herself to be a Salvadorean. As a poet and novelist her writings are noted for their clarity and profoundly sensitive representations of Central American reality. She has published several books of poetry beginning in 1943 with *Anillo de silencio (Ring of Silence)*. Her collection *Sobrevivo (I Survive)* won the prestigious Casa de las Américas Prize (Havana, Cuba) for poetry in 1978. *Suma y sigue (And Still It Goes On,* 1981), a fine anthology of her work, was prepared by Mario Benedetti. Among her novels are *Cenizas de Izalco (Izalco Ashes,* 1966*)*, written with her husband Darwin J. Flakoll, and *Album familiar (Family Album,* 1982*)*.

Carlos Aragón (b. 1950s, d. 1981), a poet and guerrilla, was known as Comandante Sebastián and served as head of the Special Forces of the FPL (Popular Liberation Forces Farabundo Martí), a member group of the FMLN. He was killed in combat. The testimony included in this book is from an interview by Paolo Martín.

Reyes Gilberto Arévalo (b. 1948) has published several books of poetry and writes about life in present-day El Salvador. The epigraph published originally with his poem that appears in this collection indicates the source of Arévalo's and his comrades' poetry. It is taken from Pablo Neruda and reads: "I speak of things that exist. God keep me / from inventing things when I sing."

Manlio Argueta (b. 1935) is one of the leading Salvadorean literary figures. He was a founding member of the University of El Salvador Literary Circle and like other writers of the Circle set off in the direction of social commitment that has led to a firm bond with the revolutionary movement. He has been dedicating his efforts to the promotion of Salvadorean and Central American Literature as a means, among other aims, of averting genocide. Now living in exile in Costa Rica, he is a prolific and internationally renowed novelist and poet. Among his novels are *Caperucita en la zona roja (Riding Hood in the Red Zone)*, which won the Casa de las Américas prize in 1977, *Un día en la vida (One day of Life,* 1981*), El valle de las hamacas (The Valley of the Hammocks,* 1970*)* and *Cuzcatlán, donde bate la Mar del Sur (Cuzcatlan, Where the South Sea Beats,* 1983*).* His poetry collections began with *Poemas* (1967) and include *Las bellas armas reales (The Beautiful Real Weapons,* 1979*).* His writings have been translated into several languages.

Paco Barrios (b. 1940) expresses in simple, popular imagery his devotion to the poor and to the idea of progress through unceasing struggle.

Nelson Brizuela (b. 1955) is developing a body of poetry characterized by a profound contemplation of the question of social responsibility and the place of poetry in a changing society. See Miguel Huezo.

Horacio Castellanos Moya (b. 1957), an editor of this collection, is one of the many accomplished young Central American poets. He was born in Honduras but his formative years were spent in El Salvador. Now living in exile in Mexico, his career is typical of his generation of poets, some of whom are attempting to establish, whenever possible, new publications dealing with Central American literature. He has published *Poemas* (1978) and is one of the poets included in the anthology *La margarita emocionante (The Thrilling Daisy,* 1979*).*

Dimas Castellón-Mariano Espinoza (b. 1950s) is an actor and dramatist whose experimental theatre aims to assist the revolutionary process in El Salvador.

Ricardo Castrorrivas (b. 1938) began working as a typist and apprentice typesetter after completing his primary education at age thirteen. His early writings won him the admiration and encouragement of Claudia Lars, Roberto

Armijo, Roque Dalton, and other poets. His collection of short stories, *Teoría para lograr la inmortalidad* (*Theory for Achieving Immortality*, 1972), established him as one of the masters of that genre in El Salvador. *Las cabezas infinitas* (*The Infinite Heads*, 1971) is an anthology containing some of his poetry. In it can be noticed the sharp satire he uses to attack the ruling system of El Salvador.

José Roberto Cea (b. 1939) was one of the most productive Salvadorean poets during the 1960s and early 1970s. In addition he prepared several anthologies of his country's poetry. His work often reflects his consciousness of the indigenous roots of Central American culture. A well-known literary figure in El Salvador, he has won important literary awards in Spain and Nicaragua. Among his books of poetry are *Todo el códice* (*The Whole Codex*, 1968), *Náufrago genuino* (*Genuine Castaway*, 1969), *Misamitin* (*Mass-meeting*, 1977). He has also written prose fiction.

Sonia Civallero (b. 1950s) is a poet and revolutionary living, as far as is known, in El Salvador.

Rolando Costa (b. 1940s) emphasizes in his poetry the idea of commitment, with a focus on class.

José María Cuéllar (1942-1981): in his several books of poetry, and until his unexplained death on a San Salvador street, Cuéllar devoted himself to the representation and service of the poor in El Salvador. The anecdotal character of his writing and his success at incorporating popular speech made his poetry widely accessible. Among his books are *Poemas* (1969); and *Crónicas de infancia* (*Childhood Stories*, 1971), which won the Venezuelan "Single Prize for Latin American Poetry" in 1972.

Roque Dalton (1935-1975) is one of the most highly acclaimed Salvadorean poets. As a founder of the University Literary Circle at the University of El Salvador, he was instrumental in uniting poetry and politics. By his example he led poets to break the silence successive dictatorships had imposed on them and to write on behalf of the denied people, in language and rhythms that readily represent their experience. The effect of firm solidarity is furthered by the testimonial character of his writings, by the integrity he brings to his consideration of the wide range of human experiences and the struggle to make a potentially beautiful world available to everyone. He was one of the founders of the People's Revolutionary Army (ERP), was jailed for his activities, escaped, and spent years in exile. After he returned to El Salvador one wing of ERP accused him of being a "Soviet-Cuban-CIA agent" and executed him after a mock trial in 1975. Fermán Cienfuegos (the poet Eduardo Sancho Castañeda), then one of the leaders of the ERP, resigned in protest to found the Armed Forces of National Resistance (FARN). Among Dalton's books of poetry are *La ventana en el rostro* (*The Window in My Face*, 1961), *El turno del ofendido* (*The Turn of the Offended*, 1964), *Poemas* (1968), *Taberna y otros lugares* (*Tavern and Other Places*, 1969), *Las historias prohibidas del pulgarcito* (*Prohibited Stories of Tom Thumb*, 1975), *Poemas clandestinos* (*Clandestine Poems*, 1975). Two very useful anthologies of his poetry are *Poesía* (1980) and *Poesía escogida* (1983). He has also written two testimonies: *Miguel Mármol* (1974); and *Pobrecito poeta que era yo* (*Poor Little Poet that I Was*, 1976). The poems in this collection are taken from *Poemas clandestinos*.

Luis Díaz (b. 1950s; presumed dead). This young writer, attempting to live, to carry on a political life, and to write in El Salvador, was seized and made one of the "disappeared" by members of the National Guard in August, 1980. He was one of the founders of the Central American Revolutionary Workers' Party (PRTC), a member group of the FMLN.

Mercedes Durand (b. 1933) has evolved as a poet from an interest in traditional themes examined by the post-modernist women poets in Spanish America to focusing on the national problem of repression. Her work is well represented in her book *Sara...la luna...la muchacha...y otros poemas (Sara...the moon...the girl...and other poems)*.

Miguel Angel Espino (1902-1967) contributed significantly in his writings to an awakening of a consciousness of the indigenous past in El Salvador.

Pedro Geoffroy Rivas (1908-1980): his daring independence, which manifested itself fruitfully in an expressive freedom characterized by conversational usages, allowed him to recognize and encourage Roque Dalton's talent. A significant part of his work was produced in exile, in Mexico. Among his books are *Canciones en el viento (Songs in the Wind)*, *Sólo amor (Only love*, 1963*)*, and *Yulcuicat* (1965).

Carlos Antonio Gómez, formerly a regime soldier, was interviewed by Ruth Fitzpatrick for the magazine *CounterSpy*, May-June 1982.

Alfonso Hernández (b. 1948): like so many of the younger Salvadorean poets, Hernández writes poetry that derives from the events in his own society. He projects an authentic Salvadorean culture that underlies and will prevail over the present oppressive phase. He is a prolific writer of books of poetry, including *Del hombre al corazón del mundo (From Man to the Heart of the World)*, Cartas a Irene (Letters to Irene) and *Poesía en armas (Armed Poetry)*. He has also published an anthology of testimonies, *León de piedra (Stone Lion*, 1982*)*.

Miguel Huezo Mixco (b. 1954): brilliant and well educated, Huezo Mixco is active in the guerrilla struggle while continuing, in difficult circumstances, to write poetry. His close colleagues are Horacio Castellanos Moya, Róger Lindo, Nelson Brizuela, and Roberto Quesada. They contribute to the books *La margarita emocionante (The Thrilling Daisy)* and *Poesía organizada (Organized Poetry)*; and publish in the journal *El papo*. His published book is *Una boca entrando en el mundo* (*A Mouth Entering the World*, 1978).

Ricardo Humano (b. 1940) is known for his conciseness of expression, and is author of the book of poetry *Dos soles en el espejo* (*Two Suns in the Mirror*).

Julio Iraheta Santos (b. 1940) writes from a Christian perspective about the suffering imposed on his country by military regimes. His book is *Confesiones para académicos y delincuentes* (*Confessions for Academics and Delinquents*, 1972).

Claudia Lars (1899-1974). Her works sometimes appear under her original name, Carmen Brannon de Samayoa. During her long and steadfast poetic career, Claudia Lars came to be known as one of the outstanding Central American poets, writing with a firm knowledge not only of the Hispanic but also of the English poetic tradition. She did not waver in her loyalty to her vocation and to her colleagues even in the face of hostile regimes, and gave great encouragement to young Salvadorean poets. In her latest poetry she wrote directly about the horrors wreaked by the Salvadorean regime in the middle 1970s. Among her numerous books are *Estrellas en el pozo* (*Stars in the Well*, 1934), *Romances de norte y sur* (*Romances from North and South*, 1946), *Escuela de pájaros* (*School for Birds*, 1955), *Canciones* (*Songs*, 1960), *Poesía última 1970-1973* (*Latest Poetry 1970-1973*, 1976). The poems in this collection are all from the section "Migajas" ("Crumbs") in *Poesía última*.

Róger Lindo (b. 1955) writes sophisticated conceptual poetry based on a commitment both to poetry and to political and military action. He has contributed along with other young poets to anthologies, and is also a painter and short story writer. See Miguel Huezo.

Mauricio Marquina (b. 1946) graduated as a doctor and wrote forceful poetry about political matters before the war of liberation created new obligations for him.

José María Méndez (b. 1916) observed the official institutions of El Salvador with a satiric eye in his prose writings. He is a former president of the National University of El Salvador. The selection here is from the book *Fliteando (Sniping)*.

Rafael Mendoza (b. 1943) is one of the founders of the literary group "Piedra y Siglo" (Stone and Century). His resourceful imagination and natural fluent expression make him one of the most attractive of Salvadorean poets. As his two poems in this collection indicate, he keeps finding novel ways, effectively using folklore and biblical motifs, to present a humane revolutionary perspective. His books of poetry include *Los muertos y otras confesiones (The Dead and other Confessions)*, *Confesiones a Marta (Confessions to Martha)*, and *Los derechos humanos (Human Rights)*.

Roberto Monterroza (b. 1945) is noted for his satiric viewing of a national situation that cries out for change. He was, with Eduardo Sancho, one of the founding members of the literary group "Las Masacuata," and has contributed to the anthology *Las cabezas infinitas (The Infinite Heads*, 1971*)*.

Nachín (b. 1946). The severity of his artistic attack on those who defend the status quo is in keeping with his full commitment to change.

Roberto Quesada (b. 1956) is one of the brilliant young poets who is fully involved in the struggle to establish a new society in El Salvador. See Miguel Huezo.

Alfonso Quijada Urías (b. 1940) became associated with the University Literary Circle founded in 1956 and is regarded as one of the leading Salvadorean poets. He knows how to articulate a variety of sentiments derived from the national reality, thoughts that were on the tips of the tongues of his progressive compatriots. Constantly engaged in furthering his country's cultural life, he currently lives in exile in Nicaragua. His books of poetry, such as *Poemas* (1967) and *Los estados sobrenaturales y otros poemas (Supernatural States and Other Poems,* 1970), as well as his collections of short stories *Cuentos* (1970) and *Otras historias famosas (Other Famous Stories,* 1976) reveal a consistently high quality of writing.

Lil Milagro Ramírez (b. 1950s; presumed dead) wrote sensitively about love in the context of the revolutionary struggle. She was captured in late 1976 and became one of the "disappeared." At the time of her capture she served as Comandante and member of the national directorate of the Armed Forces of National Resistance (FARN), a member group of the FMLN.

Salomón Rivera (b. 1948) leads an active life as poet and revolutionary.

Eduardo Sancho Castañeda (b. 1948) was, until 1970, recognized as one of the most dynamic producers and promoters of Salvadorean literature. He incorporated earlier currents of the national literary tradition, rejecting only the tendency to evade social issues. He founded journals and literary groups in various parts of El Salvador in his efforts to promote a culture of liberation. In his own poetry Sancho reveals a lively imagination and attractive formal inventiveness in dealing with great national issues. In 1971 he was one of the founders of the People's Revolutionary Army (ERP). As a result of the execution of Roque Dalton he withdrew from that group and founded the Armed Forces of National Resistance (FARN), a member group of the FMLN. After ten years of clandestine activity he surfaced in 1980 as Comandante Fermán Cienfuegos, who became one of the prominent participants in the church-mediated talks between the guerrillas and the Duarte regime in 1984-85. Sancho's works have been published in many anthologies of Salvadorean poetry, including *Las cabezas infinitas (Infinite Heads). La poesía, jodidos, la poesía (Poetry, Abused Ones, Poetry,* 1981) and *Poemas posteriores (Later Poems)* are anthologies of his poetry.

Manuel Sorto (b. 1950), one of the editors of the present collection, is active in the effort to sustain Salvadorean cultural life. He is well known as a poet and an actor, and was a member of the literary group "La Masacuata." He wrote the book of poems *Confesiones en el santuario de nuestra señora de los locos (Confessions in the Sanctuary of Our Lady of the Crazy People)*. He is living in exile in Mexico, where along with the other editors of this collection he founded the literary journal *Palo de Fuego, Cosa Centroamericana*.

Jaime Suárez Quemain (1950-1980): at the time of his kidnapping, murder, and mutilation he was editor-in-chief of the newspaper *La Crónica* and was serving on the commission for information of the Central American Revolutionary Workers' Party (PRTC), a member group of the FMLN. He participated actively in the cultural and political life of his country and wrote the book of poetry, *Sinfonía en La Menor para un recuerdo (Symphony in A Minor for a Reminiscence)*. See the selection from *La Prensa Gráfica* in this collection.

Los Torogoces de Morazán is a peasant musical group of the Oriental Front Francisco Sánchez of the FMLN.

Roberto Torres (b. 1950) is another of the poets actively dedicated to the struggle.

José Luis Valle (b. 1943) conveys in his poetry clear images of the terror imposed on the Salvadorean people. He has published several books of poetry, including *Coágulo y abismo del bien morir (Coagulation and Abyss of the Good Death)*.

Gabriela Yanes (b. 1959), one of the editors of the present collection, is developing an important body of poetry based on Salvadorean reality. She is living in exile in Mexico and working to further the cultural life of Salvadoreans and other Central Americans.